EXPEDITION
TEXAS

EXPEDITION
TEXAS

- Tales from the Road -

BOB MAULDIN

THE
History
PRESS

Published by The History Press
Charleston, SC
www.historypress.com

All images are courtesy of the author's collection.

First published 2024

Manufactured in the United States

ISBN 9781467155267

Library of Congress Control Number: 2023938568

Notice: The information in this book is true and complete to the best of our knowledge. It is offered without guarantee on the part of the author or The History Press. The author and The History Press disclaim all liability in connection with the use of this book.

CONTENTS

INTRODUCTION

It starts with a simple wrong turn down a desolate county road. A few moments later, you are among a cluster of old abandoned buildings that haven't seen life in a very long time. One appears to have been a post office. Another bears the faded paint reading "General Store" above a collapsed porch. You have stumbled upon a true Texas ghost town.

Meanwhile, a magnificent towering building looms large over the town it once served as a destination resort hotel. Its rusting spires are often obscured by low clouds, and it seems out of place among the bustling streets below. Those streets are lined with typical small-town businesses housed in structures nothing like this massive, abandoned hotel. The hotel, with its hundreds of rooms, holds even more stories. The stories of the people who came and went could fill volumes. The characters responsible for such an opulent structure have their own backstories that would warrant hundreds of pages of biography. These stories are worth being told. But they are not. These stories are being forgotten with each passing year, with the passing away of each eyewitness to history. The year is 2012. And a dad on a hike with his kids decides to change that.

Summer was doing its usual Texas best. The inescapable heat found its way into the shade, and staying indoors brought only minor relief, as the air conditioner couldn't keep up. The kids found ways to be entertained for the first few weeks of their summer vacation. The water sprinkler ran a lot and did a great job of cooling them down while keeping them active. But as summer raged on and all their adventures had been repeated to the point of boredom, the restlessness set in.

It was around that time that I found myself once again "between radio jobs," as broadcasters in a dying business often referred to our unwelcome extended vacations. Unemployment was paying the basic bills while the job search began. One particular Saturday, after finding the tenth new way of making a bologna sandwich seem appetizing to those restless kids, I sat down at the computer to see if I might have missed any job listings. Nothing. I figured that if I wanted to work in the field in which I had specialized for over a decade, I'd have to create something to do. I had no idea what that might be, and it was a frustrating process trying to picture myself happy in any of the jobs I found listed. That is when the kids showed up. The boys, in messy clothes with their sweaty red faces, had already explored the usual boring activities normally offered to them, and I could tell they had conspired to approach me.

"Can you take us on a hike in the woods?"

That question was assigned to the youngest on the merit of cuteness. The oldest elaborated to make the case. The middle one nodded and added the occasional, "Yeah!"

It did not take much convincing. I was bored with my job search and needed some time away from reality. So, we gathered some supplies, filled some water bottles and marched across the field behind the house into the nearby forest.

We had explored these woods plenty of times, but this time, we were prepared to spend the day and travel farther than before. We traversed an easy two hundred yards through trees and brush along a trail leading to the creek we intended to follow. I believed the source of this creek to be the spillway of a lake only a few miles away. When the brush was too thick, we would find a place to cross the creek using a fallen tree as a bridge. Soon, we'd have to cross again using large stones in the water. It was a fun little adventure full of navigable obstacles. At one point, about a mile into our hike, we came upon a rail bridge, supported by a massive concrete culvert. Stamped into the old cement was the date "1926." I told the boys what little I knew about the railroad as we walked through the cavernous structure. We continued following the creek until we finally arrived at the spillway to Lake Bellwood.

Lake Bellwood served as the primary source of water for the city of Tyler from 1894 to 1950. The water treatment plant and much of the recreation structures were left to ruin when the city completed construction of Lake Tyler and a new water treatment plant in 1950. Only a small portion of Lake Bellwood was accessible by car at the time of our hike. There, the ruins

A stone and cement picnic table at Lake Bellwood.

of old cement picnic tables were scattered on a hill. A small boat ramp was occasionally used by fishermen. However, the part of the lake we found, near the dam and spillway, had been left untouched for many years. Decades. The boys and I found WPA stone fire pits, more of those old cement picnic tables and other signs of family fun from days too far gone. Fallen branches and years of leaves covered most of it.

We explored a bit. Tired from our journey, and knowing we had to do it again to get home, we poked around just a little and then left. Just before leaving, I snapped a cellphone photo of my oldest son, Jacob, near the washout below the spillway. We made the hike home vowing to return. We never did.

The hike home was more routine since we had traversed these obstacles before. We didn't talk much. My mind was racing. We had just had a glimpse into pre-1950s life. We saw remnants of a time when a trip to the lake with a picnic lunch on the weekend was a real treat for the family. This wasn't ancient ruins in Rome. It wasn't a Native American camp. It wasn't the Alamo. It was a bit of everyday life for the average person living in Tyler, Texas, prior to 1950. I was fascinated. I wanted to know the stories and hear

An original water tower at Lake Bellwood.

the memories of the people who had been there. I wanted to see photos of the place in its heyday. Surely, others must be as intrigued by this as I had suddenly become.

I had dabbled in television production for a couple of years. I had produced a campy horror host program for local TV. As I walked with the boys, I began to think that if I were to approach the local station about a show exploring lost history in Texas, they might want to air it. It was only a thought. Maybe it would blow over.

It did not.

Upon emerging from the woods and crossing that field behind our house, we followed the path where earlier the eager footsteps of the would-be hiking troop had laid over a trail in the tall grass. Now, as the boys' feet dragged across that same trail, I was the eager one. I was nearly running back across that field. In the remaining hour or so of our walk back, I had conjured up the entire structure of a TV show, the business deal with the station and the sponsors and even thought up a name. I'd call it *Expedition East Texas* because, as I figured, there must be enough abandoned buildings, old graveyards and ghost towns around East Texas to do a full season of a TV show. I had recently been gifted a decommissioned news camera from that local TV station, so I knew I had the right gear to make it look good on TV.

My wife had just returned from working at an event nearby, and I am sure she wondered where we were, but she wasn't surprised when three muddy kids trudged in the front door. What might have been more surprising was that I bounded in the door with a proposition. I explained the idea and that it meant I'd need the car for a few days to produce a pilot. She looked at that decommissioned camera perched in the corner of our tiny living room, then back at me and said, "Do it!"

I had thrown out wild ideas before, so the fact that it only took one soulful pitch to get her on board with this idea meant that I was off to the races! I reached out to friends for suggestions for other lost history locations in East Texas. I went to work immediately on the pilot. It was produced within a month. I took this original episode of *Expedition East Texas* to the local station. John Gaston, the station manager, became excited and said, "Let's do it. Can you have it by this fall?" It was a stretch, but I knew I could. I created a small online presence for the show. There was an *Expedition East Texas* Facebook page and a website. As we were getting episodes together and trying to whip the local audience into a frenzy about this new local lost history show, fate played its hand.

I received an email from a man in charge of Legacy TV, a television network with digital and low-power stations across the United States. He wanted to air our TV show on his network. Of course, I wanted to do that, but he had only one request. He asked that I make the show less "regional."

"Would it be possible," he said, "to shoot stories all over Texas?"

With that, I had to entirely rethink the budget for the show, aggressively sell more sponsorships and keep the car out much longer than I had originally told my wife. The website and Facebook pages were changed to reflect the new name, *Expedition Texas*. The show went on the air in East Texas in the

Title screen for the local pilot episode of *Expedition East Texas*.

fall of 2012, and by the following spring, we had added a Dallas TV station and were upgrading our production to HD, renting studio space to edit the show and growing into more markets.

Today, *Expedition Texas* is available on stations all over the state via our own syndication and available to the rest of the country on Heartland TV Network (formerly TNN). What is more important is that for over a decade, we've traveled across the state exploring hints of Texas's colorful past. We make a point of taking our cameras into places you otherwise would never be able to explore. From the basements to the rooftops of some of the greatest old buildings in the state, to a quaint cemetery under a hundred-year-old oak tree and everything in between. We've seen a lot, but we will never see it all. This book is filled with firsthand accounts of exploring Texas's amazing lost history. It isn't necessary to have seen the TV show to enjoy the stories we share.

As actor Barry Corbin states in his introduction to our show, "Hitch a ride and travel across the Lone Star State lookin' for hints of our colorful past… our lost history. This is *Expedition Texas*…and we're gonna find it!"

Chapter 1

A MONUMENT TO MASSACRE

Malcolm Johnson held court every Saturday night at his Purple Pig Café. The Purple Pig started as a little barbecue stand, and as it grew in popularity, Malcolm added outdoor seating, which he later enclosed. When the crowds proved too big for that space, he added more outdoor seating, which he later enclosed. Now, the Purple Pig offered live music on the weekends. Being a singer/songwriter myself, I was earning some much-needed tip money playing acoustic solo sets there on the weekends. Shortly after having the idea for *Expedition East Texas*, I played one such gig and, on a break, told Malcolm of my idea for a TV show. Everyone at his table thought it was a cool idea, but Malcolm's face grew serious.

"Will you be doing ghost stories?" he asked.

"No," I said. "This is about history."

"Well, you need to do one on the Killough Monument," he explained. "Everybody says it's a haunted place, but you can avoid that part. There are a lot of stories about it, but the story of why it's there is true history."

The following weekend, with the help of a waitress from the Purple Pig, we found our way down several county roads to a dead end where, to our amazement, a stone pyramid stood nearly two stories high, surrounded by stone-covered graves. The monument memorializes a family killed as revenge for the state nullifying a treaty, angering Cherokees who were originally promised the land.

To understand the origin of the bitterness that led to the massacre, you must look at broader Texas history. The land was part of a larger portion that had originally been granted to the Cherokees under Sam Houston and John Forbes's treaty in 1836. In 1837, the Republic of Texas Senate nullified that treaty, and tracts of land were sold to early settlers. Isaac Killough Sr. and his family bought and settled on one of those tracts along what is now known as Killough Creek. Killough's family consisted of his four sons, his two daughters and their husbands. He also brought along two single men, Elbert and Barakias Williams. In early 1838, they began clearing the land, building homes and planting crops. Around the time their corn was ready to be harvested in August of that year, word was getting out that disgruntled Mexicans, having lost Texas, were conspiring to retake Texas by inciting Indian attacks on English-speaking settlers. The Mexicans, led by Vicente Cordova, hoped this would create a path for an invasion by the Mexican army, but their plans were squelched by a militia led by General Thomas J. Rusk.

More than a little concerned, Isaac Killough and about thirty other settlers fled to Nacogdoches in fear of Indian attacks. It was reported later that the Indians had agreed to allow Killough's group to return to their land and remain until the first frost. In late September, Killough's group returned, but on the afternoon of October 5, a hostile band of Indians attacked the settlement, killing eighteen of the settlers. Among them was Isaac Killough Sr.

The monument that stands at the site today was built in the 1930s by the Works Progress Administration, and in 1965, the state placed a marker detailing the events that took place there.

Our trip to Killough Monument was part of our pilot episode and was repackaged for the first episode of *Expedition Texas*. There was an eerie feeling that loomed over the location, and that had a lot to do with the way the story was relayed to us as a bit more of local legend than true Texas history. This story is both. The massacre has been local folklore to the residents of the surrounding community, so it makes sense that the Purple Pig waitress, being a lifelong resident, told it as a local ghost story. This story is an example of how larger decisions at the highest level of Texas government had a ripple effect that spread across the state. It leaves one to wonder what Texas would have looked like had Sam Houston's treaty remained intact and Texas honored its agreement with Native Americans. It's impossible to say how that might have changed the course of history, but those graves and that monument certainly would not have been part of it.

Several years after *Expedition Texas* premiered, Malcolm Johnson sold the Purple Pig, and he passed away shortly thereafter. I always found it

The Killough Monument stands among the trees near Larissa, Texas.

An arrangement of stones marks a grave at the site of the Killough Massacre.

Another view of the Killough Monument.

An inscription on the Killough Monument honors the dead.

interesting that, in addition to his barbecue offerings, he had an entire menu of traditional Native American foods. During his time there, the Purple Pig was decorated with Native American artifacts, animal skins and crafts. One seating option was a single table in a teepee erected near the restaurant. It might be said that Malcolm's interest in telling this story had less to do with ghosts and more to do with telling the story of a broken promise and how it was later avenged. Regardless of the reasoning behind the anger the Cherokees harbored, the Killoughs were simply settlers who, at that fateful time, settled on the wrong piece of land.

The descendants of the Killough family have established a foundation to provide permanent care of the property moving forward. The monument and cemetery can be found on County Road 3531 north of Jacksonville, Texas. The county road dead-ends at the monument.

Chapter 2

THE TRAIN STATION

Amarillo, Texas, is home to many lost legends and some that are very much still around. If you are one of the few who has never heard of Cadillac Ranch, you might be baffled by a collection of antique cars half-buried nose first in a field off Interstate 40. You may also be surprised to find that your urge to pull over and take pictures of the site is not only welcomed but encouraged. Oh, and if you happen to have a can of spray paint on hand, graffiti on the cars is also welcomed and somewhat expected. So much spray paint has been applied to the cars over the decades that a thick coat of plasticky paint covers every square inch of each car and in some cases provides more structure than the Detroit steel that made up the original construction.

If you are on Interstate 40 anywhere within one hundred miles of Amarillo, you will be persuaded by large colorful billboards to enjoy a "FREE STEAK" at the most famous steakhouse in Texas. Is there a catch? Of course there is! The steak is seventy-two ounces! You must eat the whole thing and a plate full of sides for it to be free. If you complete this task, you leave without paying for it and get a heaping helping of bragging rights! Don't be mistaken, though. You will pay later…with a massive case of indigestion. If you're not up for making dinner a competition against four and a half pounds of beef, you can simply enjoy a meal in a legendary tourist attraction that celebrates Amarillo's cowboy culture. A normal-sized steak here is well worth the stop, and you'll be entertained by serenading cowboy singers and the occasional competitive eater at a table on a stage trying to beat the clock and conquer the seventy-two-ounce steak meal.

The sign welcoming travelers to Amarillo, Texas.

While those things are the popular attractions for folks passing through on the interstate, the real gems of Amarillo require a bit more effort to find. The places that bring our show to town are usually abandoned and forgotten among the numerous sites Amarillo is so rightfully proud to showcase. Our first trip to Amarillo on *Expedition Texas* was to explore the Herring Hotel. The Herring was completed in 1927 and was awash in lavish beauty representative of the wealth of the city, thanks to the oil and cattle industry. The hotel hosted the rich and famous on a regular basis. Country Music Hall of Fame DJ Bill Mack once told us the story of Hank Williams staying at the Herring Hotel while in town for a tour. Bill was a young and eager DJ at the time, and seeing the opportunity to meet his idol, he called up the switchboard at the Herring Hotel and asked to ring Hank's room. He wanted to invite Hank on his radio show—which would have been a welcome invitation had it not been 5:00 a.m. when Mack placed the call. After some convincing, he was able to speak to Hank, who had been ripped from his sleep and was most likely suffering from the previous night's libations. The conversation was short and memorable, as Mack received a pretty good cussing from his country music hero.

Our tour of the Herring Hotel gave us the opportunity to explore places the general public would never see. Deep in the basement sat long-dormant boilers the size of steam locomotives. Massive wooden doors opened to cavernous rooms where food was stored. The beautiful columns in the lobby of the hotel had been hidden for decades by misguided '70s "updates" like

The once-bustling Santa Fe Depot in Amarillo, Texas.

carpeted walls and mirrors. A few of these disco-era modifications had fallen away to reveal that the columns were intact underneath.

A few years later, we were invited back to Amarillo to visit the Santa Fe Depot. Our producer at the time was certain the depot would be worth the trip, but I had reservations. I was familiar with the small depot buildings located in smaller cities around East Texas and didn't think we could fill an episode with a train station. He sent some photos, and I was intrigued enough to book the trip and check it out.

After eating a steak and spray painting an old Cadillac, we checked into the historic Barfield Hotel in Amarillo's Center City District. Like the Herring Hotel just down the road, the Barfield was built in 1927. Unlike the Herring, it has been magnificently restored. The next day, we rolled up on the Santa Fe Depot. The producer had been correct. The depot was enormous. The building is now owned by the City of Amarillo, and their intent is to preserve the building and tell its story every chance they get. Jerry Danforth, director of facilities for the city, was our guide. His knowledge of the depot's history was great, but it was enhanced by his familiarity with the inner workings of everything from the baggage scales to the steam heating system.

Top: The ticket counter at the Santa Fe Depot.

Bottom: An original luggage cart at the Santa Fe Depot.

The building was constructed in 1910 and featured a baggage and freight area, restaurant, offices, meeting spaces and, upstairs, a Harvey House Hotel. Stories of Harvey House Hotels, with their Harvey Girls and opulent accommodations, could fill a book on their own. As Jerry showed us around the depot and the hotel, the need for such a place began to make sense. He pointed out what was happening in Amarillo at the time it was built. At one point, over 80 percent of the beef in the United States was shipped out of this station. The transactions that took place over a meal in the depot were the key to the wealth that Amarillo enjoyed in the early 1900s. In some areas, the walls of this depot are three feet thick. A tunnel nearly a quarter of a mile long ran under the tracks and connected to another building nearby. This structure was state of the art in its time and is in amazing condition as it currently stands. In 2022, the City of Amarillo constructed a pavilion adjacent to the depot. The city has heard many proposals for how to make use of the original structure while preserving its many historic aspects. City leaders agree that Amarillo owes its very existence to the railroad, and the Santa Fe Depot stands as a fantastic reminder of the city's rich history.

Chapter 3

GLENRIO

No other highway feels as legendary as Route 66. In fact, much of the history mentioned when we were in Amarillo is celebrated by tourists who make trips along the original alignment of the old highway. Bypassed in favor of the interstate highway system, much of the roadway and the small towns it passes through fell by the wayside. I've long wanted to take a vacation that was nothing but traveling Route 66, but I haven't yet found anyone willing to sit in the car that long and check out small towns along the way. We had a few encounters with the Mother Road on *Expedition Texas*, but none like the one in season three.

We regularly receive suggestions from viewers with ideas for places we should visit. We investigate all of those suggestions because we have been turned on to some really amazing sites with their help. Occasionally, the idea is our own. I had wanted to visit a real Texas ghost town since the very beginning of *Expedition Texas*. We had lots of suggestions but none that I felt really had the right kind of character. I guess I had watched too many old TV shows where the happy-go-lucky travelers stumble upon a ghost town where you see the ruins of the old saloon, the sheriff's office and the general store. I guess those only exist on Hollywood back lots, because I've certainly never heard tell of one in Texas. But in our third season, we came pretty close when I stumbled upon some online photos of Glenrio, Texas…and New Mexico.

If you happened to be traveling Route 66 in the 1940s and 1950s, Glenrio would have started out as a stop on the Rock Island Railroad, but when

Route 66 came through, much of the town migrated more toward the highway than the railroad. Half of Glenrio sat in Texas and the other half in New Mexico. The federal government recognized it as a Texas town, however, and of its two post offices, mail would be dropped off at the Texas office and walked across to the New Mexico post office. Deaf Smith County on the Texas side was a dry county, so there were no bars on the Texas side of Glenrio. There were no gas stations on the New Mexico side of the town mainly because of that state's higher taxes on fuel. Glenrio was also home to what we referred to as the First/Last Motel. This is because the sign for the business read "Last Motel in Texas" if you were headed west and "First Motel in Texas" if you were traveling east.

I read everything I could find about Glenrio for weeks. I tried to find someone who could appear as a guide on the show, but that proved to be impossible as well. A weekend was set aside for travel, and it was quickly approaching. I needed a camera operator, but the two or three crew members who had helped with the show up to that point were all unavailable that particular weekend. So, it was the Glenrio episode where I gave my sons Jacob and Ryan their first jobs. Jacob was thirteen at the time and had been on set some in the past but mainly for the opportunity to travel around and explore with Dad. This time, Jacob would operate the camera. I gave him a quick training on the ins and outs of videography. Ryan was nine, but a very detail-oriented kid, so I put him in charge of making sure all the gear was loaded and taught him what all the pieces were and where they were located so he could fetch them as needed.

Now, at the time we were just really finding our footing, and I had the wise idea to buy a vehicle dedicated to shooting *Expedition Texas*. We were

Remains of the First/
Last Motel in Glenrio.

Parked along an abandoned stretch of Route 66 on the Texas side.

still barely scraping by, so I paid $1,500 for a black Ford Explorer with over 200,000 miles on it. This was the vehicle we used to travel from Tyler, Texas, to the New Mexico state line. I was worried about this, especially knowing how far we would travel between any sign of life once we hit that final stretch toward Glenrio.

When we travel to shoot the show, I typically do all the driving, but on rare occasions when I get too sleepy, I'll let one of the crew members take the wheel. That wasn't going to work with this crew of a nine- and thirteen-year-old. We set out early on a Saturday morning and hit the road headed for the Texas Panhandle. Somewhere just short of Wichita Falls, I became extremely sleepy and had to pull off the highway and take a short nap while my bored kids sat quietly. After a quick thirty minutes, I woke up feeling refreshed enough to finish the trip, and 545 miles later, we exited Interstate 40 and crossed an overpass to what appeared to be a service road. It wasn't. We had found the abandoned portion of Route 66. The road widened, and a cement median divided the lanes. A true sign of the location, a tumbleweed merrily bounced across the road in front of the car. I thought that would make an excellent shot for the show, so we backed up the car and grabbed the camera. Ryan retrieved the tumbleweed and ran back across the road with it. When I called "action," he released the tumbleweed into the wind, and it bounced across the road again…right behind the camera. Ryan chased the tumbleweed down at least half a dozen times, and finally we managed to somewhat re-create the path it had taken when we arrived in Glenrio. Had it not been a ghost town, there surely would have been folks wondering what the crazy East Texas family was doing playing with a tumbleweed in the road.

Glenrio did not disappoint. The downtown street of Route 66 looked perfectly preserved against the desert backdrop. The Texas side of the city

Bob exploring an abandoned building in Glenrio.

and the road were just as we had seen in photos taken by other travelers. The First/Last Motel bore a slight resemblance to its postcard days. The old post office and gas station were still standing, along with a few other buildings we could not identify. For the show, I did my best to share the knowledge I had gained from my research, while Jacob struggled to keep the camera steady against some strong winds that beat on the old town constantly. Though it was a little too cold for them to be out, Ryan searched for rattlesnakes. Thankfully, he did not find one.

These days, at the New Mexico state line, the town and the pavement for Route 66 ends. The once-bustling highway becomes a dirt road at this point and shoots across the desert to the west as far as the eye can see. Just to the north, you can see the passing cars and hear the roar of Interstate 40. Eerily reminiscent of the Disney film *Cars*, this was a Route 66 town that died when the interstate highway passed it by. People quit coming. They didn't need to. They were zooming west with no need to slow down.

Chapter 4

THE GALVESTON BREWERY

If you've ever pulled a tab on a can of Falstaff Beer, odds are you grew up with the brand and for some reason turned away from it after the mid-1960s. Falstaff was once a top brand and had breweries in multiple states. In fact, it was the first brewer to operate in more than one state. In 1956, Falstaff came to Texas.

The local Galveston-Houston Brewing Company in Galveston had been in operation since the late 1800s. Its facility was originally constructed with large arched openings where its High-Grade beer was loaded on horse-drawn wagons to be transported to customers across the region. During Prohibition, the brewery made other beverages, but by the 1950s, Falstaff had its eye on the location. Upon purchasing the property, Falstaff added to the brewery with multiple enormous cement buildings housing the equipment to keep up with the demand for thousands of barrels of beer across the southern United States. Brewing took place in a tower that for decades was the tallest building on the island. Massive kettles were housed on each floor, and as the process moved forward, the product would make its way down the tower until it reached the lower floors brewed and ready for the next step. A separate multilevel building was lined on every floor with copper kettles. These copper kettles were where the brew, known at this stage as wort, would ferment while being carefully monitored by technicians. Once the proper fermentation and aging was achieved, the beer was off to a portion of the complex known as the bottling works. Atop

A historic photo of the old Galveston Brewery, which later became Falstaff.

the fermenting plant, a lounge was perched on the rooftop overlooking Galveston. Here, the company could hold beer tastings and schmooze distributors and visitors touring the plant. Of course, there was always the freshest Falstaff Beer on tap.

Our first visit to the brewery came three decades after the brewery closed in 1981. In 2012, it was our first season of *Expedition Texas*, and up until this episode, each episode had featured multiple locations told in shorter, more concise segments. This was the building that changed that formula. There was so much to see that we literally spent hours exploring the place. In the early days, our way of shooting was what I like to call "run and gun," where the camera operator is basically another adventurer and you're seeing the tour as it happens from his or her perspective. While this puts the viewer in the moment, it can also give you a headache. It's not easy to watch. However, with a lot of editing, we managed to take our audience through the entire building. The 1950s additions to the original brewery were historic in their own right, but one of the most fascinating things about this factory was that it was basically built around, and on top of, the original 1890s structure. So, with a knowledgeable guide, you could find original portions still intact and preserved amazingly well within the walls of the concrete behemoth. Original wooden window frames with their original glass sat between sections of the building. The brick arched openings of the original loading dock were also tucked neatly inside. Much of the original building sat complete within the more modern design of the 1950s upgrades.

A gentleman named Ralph Stenzel owned the building in 2012 when we came to visit. How one man came to own a closed-down factory is a story in itself, and that particular tale ended up on the cutting room floor, left out of that episode. Ralph's memories of the building in its heyday were firsthand knowledge, which made his telling all the more appealing. As he told of what happened in each room of the building, you could almost picture it humming with productivity, crawling with workers and filling the air with the smell of freshly brewed beer. Reality was not quite as nice. The smell was instead that of musty, moldy walls dripping with moisture. The sea air has not been kind to the exposed frame in some parts of the building, and once-strong beams of American steel now held on by rusty threads. The copper kettles that once filled the fermenting facility had been looted long ago with their valuable metal being sold by the pound and no thought given to their historical significance. The post-apocalyptic look of the place would have made a great sci-fi or horror film set. Still, the building left a lasting impression and set the bar high for future episodes. It set the bar so high, in fact, that it became one of those future episodes. In 2022, ten years later, we went back.

Bob explores the interior of the Falstaff Brewery in Galveston.

Jerome Karam is a visionary. It takes a visionary to drive by the ruins of the Falstaff Brewery as it sat ominously against a cloudy sky and somehow see something beautiful. The Falstaff had been vacant nearly forty years. It had survived multiple hurricanes. In many of these buildings, folks like to say "the bones are strong" to imply they are worthy of keeping. The "bones" of this building would flake off in your hand. When I had sailed out of the nearby port on a cruise in June 2022 and saw construction equipment around the building, I thought surely they were in the process of tearing it down. I couldn't have been more wrong. Later that summer, we were preparing to shoot episodes where we revisited sites from our first season. I figured I might have a chance to shoot in the Falstaff plant one last time before the place was leveled. So, imagine my surprise when my research turned up the name of a company that planned to restore the building and turn it into a world-class hotel! JMK5 Holdings has a track record of taking derelict properties and turning them into useful real estate. Jerome Karam leads a team of architects, subcontractors and interior designers who swarmed the Falstaff complex and formed a plan to see Jerome's vision come to life.

When we returned to Falstaff ten years later, we found the old fermentation building had been converted into climate-controlled indoor self-storage. High above, the tasting room had been completely restored to historically accurate detail and now hosted events on a regular basis. The vast shipping and receiving areas were now being utilized as indoor port parking for travelers cruising out to sea. In the tower and the original bottling works areas of the plant, efforts were being made to replace rotted steel beams with brand-new treated beams designed to last at least one hundred more years. Floors were being leveled and rooms were being designed around the original architecture. We toured areas that were oddly familiar but now renewed with fresh materials to prepare for life as a luxury hotel.

The Falstaff Brewery isn't the first place we've seen reemerge during our ten-year run. The Statler Hotel in downtown Dallas was completely abandoned when we visited it in 2013, but in 2021, my wife and I were able to stay there in a room I'm quite sure we explored when it was a crumbing ruin. The comeback was amazing for the Statler Dallas, but what sets the restoration of Falstaff apart is that it isn't simply a restoration and remodel. The Falstaff building is a complete reimagining of the structures that made up the complex. From covered parking and climate-controlled storage to a fine hotel and an event center, JMK5 Holdings made perfect use of each building in a way that is best suited to its original design. In the future, there will be a trip planned and we'll stay in a room at a hotel that was once the brewery that made famous Falstaff Beer.

Chapter 5

SS *SELMA*

'm no engineer. The largest thing I ever built was a doghouse for my dog Jake, and he hated it. With those credentials, I really have no place criticizing a design by actual engineers that was funded and constructed by the U.S. government—but a concrete ship? Really? I really shouldn't cast stones, but I certainly wouldn't build a boat out of them!

Apparently, there came a time when a shortage of materials made it necessary for the U.S. government to experiment with different materials to build ships. The material they settled on was concrete. Yes, these ships floated. They served our interests during the First World War. They were less expensive to build, using steel only as framing and the concrete to fill in the gaps. The largest of the concrete ships ever to be built was the SS *Selma*, built in 1919 and launched on June 28 of that same year. That was the same day as the signing of the Treaty of Versailles by Germany putting an end to the war, meaning the ship never saw wartime use. It served as an oil tanker the remainder of its career.

SS *Selma* was built in Mobile, Alabama, but named in honor of Selma, Alabama. This ship served just under a year. The *Selma* hit a jetty near Tampico, Mexico, in May 1920. The accident ripped a massive hole in its hull. Attempts at repairs proved unsuccessful, and the massive ship was scrapped just off Pelican Island near Galveston.

We came to know about SS *Selma* when viewers repeatedly told us to explore the "sunken ship" near Galveston. At the time, we had been in production only a couple of years and were in no way prepared to produce

A historic photo of the SS *Selma* during its service.

an underwater episode. I'd simply tell them, "Thanks. Maybe later." I don't recall exactly how we discovered that a large surface of the ship's deck was still above sea level and available to explore, but it certainly led to me trying to find a way to reach it.

Some amount of thought must go into planning each of our expeditions. Typically, this is only a small amount of coordination between property owners and maybe a guide. In the case of the SS *Selma*, we needed to be able to get out into the bay and onto the ship and do so without our guide. Not many were willing to step aboard the *Selma* due to its condition. So we planned to stop off at Pier 21 to visit Jamie White, the director of the Texas Seaport Museum. There we learned all the facts about SS *Selma* before venturing out on our own to find the ship. Getting to the ship itself required a bit more coordination with Caribbean Breeze Boat rentals and the adventurous Captain J.J., who piloted his boat, the *Trouble Maker*, right up to the hull of the SS *Selma*.

I don't know what I expected to see when we tied off to the *Selma*, but this wasn't it. Very little concrete remained. The ship was mostly rusted rebar with crumbling chunks of cement holding it together. The rebar, as we referred to in the show, was made up of steel bars that have started to succumb to the pressures of the salty sea water and occasional tropical storms. Where the waters of the high tide cover the ship's barely recognizable deck, a film of thick, slippery algae has coated the slanted surface, meaning you're skating down a jagged surface with rusty metal spikes protruding just below the water's surface. Of all the places we've been that I've had to warn viewers about, this is the most serious. Do NOT try to board the *Selma* as we foolishly did in 2015. As we walked along the deck, there were occasional human-sized holes in the surface where one would guess unwitting adventurers fell to their demise. I could find no such reports, and Captain J.J. laughed off the assumption.

Below the deck, in areas that had caved in over time, you could see openings to the rooms that crew members occupied. A few of these rooms were filled with water, and from the surface, you could see enormous schools of tiny fish churning up the water as they swam in circles. Huge wooden beams held strong as cross supports for the ship. All seemed to hold strong—except the concrete, which I'm afraid our 1919 counterparts overestimated as a building material. With each step, more and more of the SS *Selma* crumbled into the black stagnant water below. We crept carefully back to the *Trouble Maker* and started our journey back to Pier 21. As the little boat hopped across the bay, we were escorted away from the SS *Selma* by three or four dolphins that found our presence as amusing as we did theirs.

I can't leave this chapter without mentioning Matt Morton. Matt has been a recognizable name over the East Texas radio airwaves for the better part of three decades. In fact, when I was unceremoniously fired from one of my radio jobs, it was my friend Matt who took my place as the host of my old show. Matt is one of the most tried and true friends anyone could ever

A view of the SS *Selma* from our chartered boat.

Bob and Captain J.J. on the deck of the SS *Selma*.

hope for. He is the kind of friend who keeps in touch no matter what is going on in his life. Everyone needs a Matt Morton in their lives. On this trip, we found ourselves short of a camera operator, and I offered the spot to Matt and told him that I would train him prior to the shoot. He took me up on it and traveled to Galveston with me for the shoot. Matt still talks about that adventure to this day. Every dangerous step Captain J.J. and I took in that episode was taken moments before by Matt Morton, hauling a heavy camera rig on his shoulder and doing his best not to create one of those ominous human-sized holes in the deck of the *Selma* to those black waters below. Thank you, Matt. We'll go back. Someday.

Chapter 6

NEWGULF

There is something eerily fascinating about entering a location where it seems the world stopped decades before and everything is still somewhat in its place. This was the case in one of our first expeditions. Newgulf was a town built around a sulfur mine. This was a true company town where all the residents were also employees of the only business in town. The mine and the sulfur it produced were king. Offices, laboratories, the post office and even the vaults were all part of daily life in Newgulf...until they weren't.

As we planned the first season of *Expedition Texas*, I ran across photos of an abandoned sulfur mining operation in Wharton County known as Newgulf. There were some unrecognizable structures in the photos, a couple of pictures of an old smokestack, several office buildings and a huge warehouse still standing as recently as a few years before I discovered the photos. In many of the historic locations we visit, there's some sort of museum or historical society with information that is useful in telling the story. Occasionally, there's even a willing guide to take us to the site. Sometimes, though, they are not so willing.

A.C. Shelton was, by all accounts, the resident expert on Newgulf. According to our research, A.C. grew up in the company town and even spent a significant part of his life working at the plant. Through a few phone calls, I wound up on the phone with A.C. What we were trying to accomplish with *Expedition Texas* was a new concept at that time. A.C. didn't understand why we wanted to do a story on a closed-down mining operation.

A view of the Texas Gulf mining operation at Newgulf.

"There's nothing out there," he argued.

"Well, I've seen recent pictures of abandoned buildings and warehouses," I countered.

"Well, why would you want to see that?!"

"Because that's what the show is about!"

A.C. finally agreed to show us around despite thinking we were crazy for wanting to see the ruins of his former workplace and home. The resulting episode could barely contain all the unique features of this fascinating place.

In 1928, Newgulf, Texas, was founded as the company town for Texas Gulf Sulphur Company. The operation sat on the largest sulfur deposit in the world and drew in workers from all over the country. At one time, there were over four hundred homes in the residential area of the town and fifteen businesses in the downtown area. Around 1940, the population peaked at just over 1,500 residents. By the time we visited in 2012, most of the homes in the company town were gone. They had been moved away from the location but can still be spotted all over Wharton County. There was still plenty to see at the location of the Texas Gulf Sulphur Company. Half a dozen buildings were arranged just inside a gate, and our guide, A.C., had the key.

We met A.C. on a very hot summer day. Whatever reluctance he had prior to our visit melted away as he began to show us around his old workplace. It was a pleasant trip down memory lane for him as we traversed quickly through some of the large buildings at the plant. We had to ask him to slow down many times so that the camera could get into position. There were thousands of clues to the plant's productive days, but none more amazing than those found in the accounting office and the laboratory.

A.C. Shelton worked in accounting at the plant when it was in operation, so when we walked into that particular building, he had much more

A.C. Shelton holding a hard drive used to store data from the accounting department at Newgulf.

information to share. As he passed through a cluttered room with gold low-pile carpet, he bent over to pick up a large round object with a handle and a plug on one side. The object resembled the lid to a large garbage can.

"This was a hard drive!" said A.C.

"A hard drive? For a computer?" I asked.

"Yes! It held 20 megs. Not gigs. MEGS!" Even A.C. laughed at the thought. "Every day at the end of work, someone had to take it down to the bank and dump it on their system so we could use it the next day."

In another building, early desktop computers sat on desks with three decades of dust settled between their keys. Down a long hallway was the laboratory where all the sulfur was tested. It truly appeared as though when the five o'clock whistle blew on that final day in 1993, everyone dropped what they were doing and went home and never returned. Jars of unused chemicals remained in old refrigerators that hadn't powered up in decades. Complex machines used to test sulfur sat dormant. A light layer of yellow dust coated everything. Dated samples seemed eerily expectant of lab results that would never come.

We toured the buildings at a near-frantic pace. Our camera operator, Joe Silva, desperately tried to keep up. In those early days, we just shot everything as it happened. We learned from those early shoots that we needed to slow down and plan our shots rather than just try to capture the tour as it happens. Especially when our guide is as energetic and excited

The bus stop is all that remains in downtown Newgulf, Texas.

about revisiting the past as A.C. Shelton turned out to be—with a little convincing, of course.

In 2022, we went back to Newgulf and with a new guide saw several places we overlooked on our previous visit. We visited a large bus stop on the old downtown main street that was once the center of activity in Newgulf. Since our last visit, the plant itself had come under private ownership, and we were not permitted to visit what was left there.

Chapter 7

THE BAKER HOTEL

Some abandoned buildings are so large they cannot fit into a single episode of *Expedition Texas*. There is so much history and so much to see that you simply cannot stand to leave pieces on the cutting room floor. Such is the case with the Baker Hotel in Mineral Wells, Texas.

The Baker Hotel once stood as the lone skyscraper west of Fort Worth. In fact, it is still the only thing scraping the sky around Mineral Wells. The namesake for the hotel, Theodore Brasher Baker, gained fame for building some of the most opulent hotels in the country, including the Baker Hotel in Dallas and Hotel Texas in Fort Worth, and he worked as manager of the Connor Hotel in Joplin, Missouri. For the Baker Hotel in Mineral Wells, the people of the town wanted to pull out all the stops and build a hotel worthy of the shareholders and visitors to the highly profitable home of the curative Crazy Water there. In fact, the Olympic-sized swimming pool Baker insisted on building right in front of the hotel was filled with that famous Mineral Wells water.

Besides its breathtaking beauty, enormous size and seemingly out-of-place location, the Baker Hotel was noteworthy for other reasons. To begin with, that pool Baker wanted so badly resulted in the Baker being the first hotel in Texas to have one. The hotel was resplendent with beautiful arches and shapely ornamental trim work that gave the space a palatial feel. The cloud ballroom atop the Baker Hotel played host to all the largest touring acts of the time. The Baker Hotel Spa was a major attraction for visitors. After all, the reason folks were coming to the city in droves was

A historic postcard view of the Baker Hotel in Mineral Wells, Texas.

that fantastic healing mineral water. Brochures for the hotel spa showed cartoon characters entering the Baker tired and beaten down only to leave refreshed and rejuvenated.

Our visit to the Baker Hotel in 2013 was the largest, most daunting expedition we had undertaken to date. This was still in our run-and-gun shooting days, where we would simply do our best to keep up with the guide and see what we had later at the studio when we edited. The footage wasn't great. Longtime friend Joe Silva had returned to camera duties at that time. He would be the first to tell you that he was not a camera operator, but as mentioned previously, I pulled him into action on several occasions. Joe made a living installing satellite TV systems at that time and happened to have a weekend off when we needed to shoot at the Baker. He agreed to hit the road again. We were there all day.

We were met by Laird Fairchild and Chad Patton, two of the principal partners who had recently bought the old hotel with full intentions of bringing it back to its former glory. The two men were infinitely knowledgeable about the hotel, including subtle locations as specific as the false wall in a corner pantry that led to a cubby where Baker stored his illegal (at the time) booze. In the living space of Baker's apartment, near the fireplace, the guys led me to a spot where I inadvertently stood on the very spot where Baker was found dead. I quickly took a step back.

We tend to explore these locations from top to bottom. Basements are as interesting as bell towers. In most cases, the basements and subbasements are more interesting than anything else in the building. A basement tends to be the place where all the spare parts are stored. Extra doors, light fixtures, replacement parts, tools, old decorations and repair materials are usually stored exactly where they were left when the building closed. This is why we always pack lights in our gear, because often in buildings with no electricity, the basement is dark as night and holds hazards unseen without some illumination. Add the need to film, and you'd better have something

Our most recent trip to Mineral Wells shows work at the Baker Hotel ongoing.

to cut through the darkness. This was the case when we took a turn down a stairwell that Chad Patton told us led to the "large, dark and spooky" basement below.

After following our camera lights down the stairs to the basement, we began to hear water running. It sounded like a large amount of water. Much of the basement area had standing water throughout. Some of the city's water mains ran under the Baker and through this very area. It turns out that a city water line was broken and leaking in the basement, which meant a call to the city was in order and our basement tour was cut a little short. Fortunately, it did not end before we found ourselves in a spot that very few had ever seen in the history of the Baker Hotel. Our path out of the basement led us right *under* the massive swimming pool at the hotel. It was empty, of course, but being in that position was one of the most fascinating places we'd ever stumbled upon. We didn't have to stumble much. I'm quite sure Chad took us there on purpose to help build excitement about this place.

Chad and Laird were already excited. What our viewers saw as a crumbling piece of Texas history, these men saw as opportunity. To do what they wanted meant millions upon millions of dollars had to be raised. It meant years of wrangling for historic tax credits and grants. It meant finding investors who shared their vision and didn't see the Baker as a towering liability. They found and accomplished all of those things.

The last time we visited Mineral Wells, the Baker was swarming with activity. Construction was ongoing, and the building was showing definite signs of rejuvenation. As they say on their actively updated website, the Grand Old Lady will return.

According to that website, "The Baker Hotel Development Partners, LLC and its affiliates—in conjunction with support from the city of Mineral Wells—will revive the 14-story Spanish Colonial Revival tower to feature a fully-renovated collection of 165 guest rooms and amenities—including a spa, convention and business facilities, event ballrooms, and restaurant, coffee shop and retail options. The local mineral springs that once drew celebrities from around the world will be utilized again, along with modernized amenities adapted to the lifestyle of the modern-day guest. Blending historic architectural design with new technology, the hotel will offer expanded guest rooms and gracious public spaces to host weddings, special events, conventions and the sojourning weekenders." We can't wait to visit! You can follow the progress at bakerhotelandspa.com.

We cannot talk about the Baker Hotel and not talk about the resulting relationship that developed with the City of Mineral Wells in the ensuing years.

We revisited Mineral Wells for the fall 2020 season of the show. On that visit, we toured Crazy Water with owner Carol Elder. The mineral water that brought people to Mineral Wells from all over the country is still flowing. The Famous Water Company bottles that water and makes it available in stores all over the region. A steady stream of visitors stops by to refill their personal containers with the water and to buy souvenirs of their visit to the home of Crazy Water.

On that same visit, we explored another famous hotel. The Crazy Water Hotel was just as magnificent as the Baker Hotel but lacked the ornate architecture that made the Baker seem so incredible. However, at the time of our visit, significant progress had been made at restoring the hotel. By the time we returned in 2023 to deliver remarks at the Mineral Wells Chamber Banquet, the hotel was complete and open for business. The event was held in the restored pavilion shopping area, and we were treated to accommodations on the fourth floor in a room that resembled a one-bedroom apartment. A coffee bar and a taproom were located on the first floor, and the downtown area was bustling with activity. As this growth continues, Mineral Wells is laying the foundation to become a bustling backdrop for the Baker Hotel when it returns. As a symbol of

The restored entrance to the Crazy Water Hotel.

the community, its birth is thanks exclusively to the mineral water that made the city famous. It's that water that inspired generations to pursue health and wellness. With that in mind, a campaign was mounted to have the city named the Wellness Capital of Texas. That honor was officially bestowed upon the city in 2023, and it has become a moniker the city will be known by for years to come. *Expedition Texas* will be a part of making that distinction since Mineral Wells Chamber of Commerce has partnered with our show as a sponsor.

Chapter 8

THE BRANCH DAVIDIANS
OF WACO

There is nothing that I can write here about what happened over the course of fifty-one days in 1993 that hasn't already been covered from every possible angle imaginable on larger platforms than a book about the travels of a little TV show. Movies, documentaries, books and websites covered this story, and it is still current and relevant. It is consumed and talked about as much today as it was thirty years ago. I won't try to recount the history. The short retellings we've offered in previous chapters would do this no justice. This chapter is about visiting a place so closely associated with modern history that it has largely been left untouched since the news cameras left. Those left behind picked up the pieces, but they didn't get them all. What remains on the site of Mount Carmel near Waco, Texas, is a haunting reminder of the lives lost and, depending on your stance, a possible overreach by the U.S. government that caused the deaths of David Koresh and his followers. Our show, this book and our team take no sides on what happened there. Any information relayed in this chapter comes straight from the survivor we met who showed us the ruins of the Branch Davidian compound.

Chris Moore, our show's story producer, was busy pitching ideas in 2018. One of those ideas involved traveling to the site of the Branch Davidian compound to do a story. With our focus on buildings and locations we can actually tour on our show, I questioned his idea. It wasn't that the story wasn't truly fascinating to me, but what was there to *see*? We need to show our viewers something when we tour a location. I was afraid we would

Fire destroys the Branch Davidian compound near Waco, Texas.

be standing in an open field pointing to an empty spot where the famous compound once stood and just telling what happened there. As stated, we have no interest in trying to tell that story.

Chris continued to pitch the idea and began to do some research. It turned out that a Branch Davidian named Charles Pace returned to the site after the furor had settled and had been working to memorialize the lives lost there and even built a chapel to continue in the ministry that was once at the center of the Branch Davidians.

To be clear, David Koresh did not start the Branch Davidians. "David Koresh" wasn't even his name. His given birth name was Vernon Howell. The story of this offshoot of the Seventh-day Adventist Church started long before Howell was even born. In 1935, a man named Victor Houteff started what was called the General Association of Davidian Seventh-day Adventists, and later, a continuation of that church was started by Benjamin Roden. Through a long and winding tale of church splits, prophecies unfulfilled, death and later a "snatching up of loose reins," David Koresh became the self-proclaimed leader of the movement, and what followed was a series of apocalyptic messages and the purchase of a vast array of weapons both legal and illegal to fortify the compound at Mount Carmel. This summarizes nearly fifty years of history into a nice, simple story to get us to 1993 and what began to happen there. As has been told ad nauseum, the weapons being shipped led to warrants and the initial raid, which led to the subsequent standoff. Lives were lost. Negotiations were a mess. Tactics were used to try to flush out the Davidians, and when those didn't work, more violent means were employed. As the government agents tired of broken promises from Koresh, they began assaulting the building using the muzzles of tanks and inserting tear gas in the building. Depending on who you believe, either the tear gas cannisters sparked a fire *or* the Davidians holed up inside set the place on fire, and soon it was a smoldering pile of ashes on an otherwise beautiful piece of Central Texas land. The aftermath of these fifty-one days left four ATF agents dead and another sixteen wounded. Six Branch Davidians died in the initial raid, and an astonishing seventy-six of them remained with Koresh until the very end, dying in the horrific flames.

Charles Pace was living at the Mount Carmel compound when producer Chris Moore began to try to make contact. We didn't expect him to want to talk and were surprised to receive an eager, friendly invitation. Jeff Miller, a very experienced videographer and frequent camera operator for *Expedition Texas*, was very interested in shooting this episode. Chris came along for the shoot for one of the first times. Along for the ride, and to make sure my shirt was tucked in when it needed to be, was my soon-to-be wife, Tessa. We all had more than a passing interest in what had happened on the property, as the images were seared into our memories. For an episode of the show, I didn't have high hopes. I didn't expect viewers to care about a tiny new building in a field where the compound once stood. What we found when we arrived wasn't that at all. This tour was one of the most surprising and heartbreaking of my career.

Sometime before we came, Charles had suffered a stroke and was confined to a motorized scooter. We met with him in the new chapel, and he gave us a fascinating interview about the history of the Branch Davidians and who David Koresh really was. According to Charles, he was originally a Branch Davidian but had left after warning Koresh of the dangers of playing God with his followers. Both Koresh and Pace knew that a battle was coming and seemed to predict the impending siege. Not long after things calmed down in Texas, Charles came back and began the process of healing Mount Carmel. He memorialized those who were lost. Their names can be found engraved on stones around the land. He also memorialized the ATF agents who lost their lives there. The interview and Charles's words were haunting, mainly because so much of what he said matched up with an image in my own memory of the time. I finally understood what it is like for our viewers when we cover a subject from their own memory.

Charles's wife, Alex, took over the tour after we interviewed Charles. We were led outside to view what remained of the original compound. A water standpipe constructed near a well had stored the water for the compound when it was inhabited by Davidians. The base of that standpipe and the well remained. A large cement pool that had been under construction during the days before the siege was still there and partially filled with murky water collected from occasional rains. More disturbing was the tunnel that had been beneath the building.

I sometimes catch myself being a bit bossy on set, and if I see a shot I want, instead of trying to explain what I want, I grab the camera and shoot it myself. This was the case when I grabbed the camera from Jeff Miller and lowered it through a small opening in the ground into a caved-in tunnel near the base of the compound. I could see—and, later, the audience watching on TV could see—the underground chamber leading to a buried school bus. As I did this, I was informed by Alex that this bunker of sorts was where many of the seventy-six Branch Davidians died during the fire. I quickly pulled the camera out of the hole and stepped back. My whole mood about the place changed. Regardless of how I felt about the details of the story before or since, this was a place where people, loyally following a leader they felt truly cared for them, had ultimately perished in the most horrific way possible—fire. I still didn't fully understand the horror of that location at the time. It wasn't until a flurry of new films were released in 2023 and I saw a reenactment of what those last moments held in that tunnel that I truly regretted lowering the camera into the opening in the ground. So many of our stories are about the places people worked or where someone did something we've read about in a history book. They are almost never about a place where so many people lost their lives in a fiery, painful way.

Everyone has an opinion of David Koresh, and everyone is entitled to that. Many followers of a new religion have that moment when they are excited about the revelations they receive. Some take it too far. Koresh was enticed to come learn from the original Davidians and learned their doctrines. He then took what he learned from them, put himself above the religion and placed himself in a position to be worshiped. I understand that there are still groups among the Davidians who believe Koresh and the followers that perished that day will be coming back. To them, I have to say that I'm sorry for feeling the way I do. From everything we have learned, he only sought to elevate himself, and he took many of your friends and loved ones from this world with him to glorify himself. If I am someday proven wrong, I'll admit that and change my tune. Many people died following a *man*. He wasn't divine. He performed no miracles. He healed no people. He only hurt them. He ultimately killed them.

I don't share my opinion often. This is the only time that a story on this show personally affected me. Most of what we cover is fun and interesting. We are supposed to learn fun facts and trivia from this show.

In the final shot of this episode, we're walking down a dirt road at the back of the property. In that shot, Alex is telling us about the agents who had taken over a bunkhouse there and used it for their assault on the compound. As we are shooting that scene, I'm seeing a corroded shell casing peeking out of the dirt in the road.

I make a mental note of the location.

Jeff Miller calls, "Cut!"

As we walk back, I let Alex get ahead of me. I find the casing and scoop it out of the dirt: "223"—government issue.

It rides with me to this day.

Chapter 9

OLD HIGHWAY 80

Did you get your kicks on Route 66? I hope so. We're not talking about that highway at all during this chapter. Yes, there is a portion of what is referred to as the Mother Road that runs through Texas, and we talk about it a little in previous chapters of this book. What we want to talk about here is the highway that once crossed Texas and brought famous faces to the Texans who were lucky enough to pick up their local newspaper and catch word of their arrival.

We can't talk about Highway 80 without first discussing the Bankhead Highway. The Bankhead Highway dates to 1916 and followed a path that later became Highway 80 and Highway 67 in Texas. A trip along the Bankhead could prove to be confusing, as many of the original alignments are unmarked and lost to time. In many locations through West Texas, you'll find original portions of the Bankhead Highway near a stretch of old Highway 80, all bypassed by Interstate 20. In fact, the towns of Ranger, Eastland and Cisco thought so much of the Bankhead Highway and what it brought to their cities that they paved portions of the road in beautiful red Thurber bricks. In a recent jaunt off I-20 during a photo-taking trip for this book, I explored Ranger. I followed one of those brick portions of the old Bankhead far out of town and into the country. I marveled at just how much of this road remained. Along this stretch of road, just outside town, was the state historical marker for the discovery of an oil well that set Ranger up for its boom and caused its original explosion in growth.

The westernmost spot on the former Highway 80 in Texas, just a few steps east of the New Mexico state line.

Later, Highway 80 bypassed the Bankhead Highway but only a block south. Ranger continued to flourish. It wasn't until I-20 bypassed Ranger by a wide stretch that the once booming little town slowly found its way to ruin. Bits of the old Bankhead are scattered across Texas, but they are becoming increasingly hard to find. You can still find your way to bits of the abandoned roadway by exploring Eastland, Cisco, Ranger and Abilene, among others.

A rich, more recent history can be found along the original path of Highway 80. We had a chance to explore old Highway 80 over the course of three episodes in 2014, and even though the highway doesn't truly exist west of Dallas, we were able to explore key locations along the original alignment of U.S. 80.

Highway 80 stretches from Tybee Island, Georgia, to San Diego, California, and was advertised as the "first coast to coast all-weather route for auto travelers." At one time, more cars were recorded entering California on U.S. 80 than rival U.S. 66. As far as Texas is concerned, the sheer number of stories along the Texas portion of the road would fill volumes. There are numerous episodes of *Expedition Texas* that connect to U.S. 80 in some way. Tales of Bonnie and Clyde come up frequently in connection to locations along the road, although the infamous pair was known to stay off the main thoroughfares.

You are far more likely to hear stories of Elvis Presley and Johnny Cash when talking about Highway 80. This has a great deal to do with the location of two major stops that made up the earliest dates of their careers, along with a wide array of other early stars of *Louisiana Hayride* in Shreveport and the *Big D Jamboree* in Dallas. Connecting those two major country music shows was a stretch of U.S. 80 that passed through East Texas and most notably Gladewater, Texas, where a celebrated country radio DJ named Tom Perryman had taken up promoting shows as another source of revenue for his growing family.

A brick portion of the old Bankhead Highway near Ranger.

Near the old Bankhead Highway is a renumbered portion of Highway 80.

From 2001 to 2011, I worked with Perryman in his post-retirement stint at KKUS radio in Tyler and often heard the stories he'd tell of Elvis's stay at the Res-Mor Motel and his meager ninety-dollar payday at the Mint Club. Tom told of Elvis and his band—at the time consisting of just a guitar player and a bass player—being low on funds and needing to pick up a date to get gas money to travel from Shreveport to Dallas for the *Big D Jamboree*. As their old car limped into Gladewater on fumes, Tom made arrangements with the Mint Club and quickly promoted Elvis's appearance there. Normally, as a promoter/booking agent, Tom would take a cut of the door, but when it turned out to be only ninety dollars, Perryman let Elvis keep it all. It's been told that Elvis never forgot it.

In our sixth season on TV, Tom led us through some of those storied locations with the help of a cane and an encyclopedic mind that held firsthand stories of country and early rock music. We started off in the old KSIJ radio studio that sat atop the T.W. Lee building along Highway 80. The radio studio still maintained the original layout, but the radio equipment was long gone. Tom sat surrounded by the polycylindrical walls of the "live room" to recount the incredible stories that took place there.

Later, he ambled up to the old Res-Mor Motel and into the room where Elvis once stayed. Tom made a joke about the number of girls who must have visited there. We found what was purported to be the building that housed the Mint Club and the stage where Elvis must have played. There were conflicting stories about the building, and the owner had no idea what the building once housed. A quick comparison of the photos from Elvis's Gladewater gig and what was left of the stage in the old building pretty much confirmed it for us, but the reports of trusted local historians had us questioning our findings about the Mint Club.

What we know without a doubt is that the places Tom Perryman showed us were authentic, and there's something extremely fascinating about retracing steps from over sixty years earlier with a man who had so much influence in country and early rock music from a tiny town in East Texas. Because of our years working together and Tom's influence in my own career, he and his wife, Billie, became like a set of bonus grandparents to me. It was a sad day for everyone when he passed away at the age of ninety in 2018. He recorded many of his stories and shared many cherished photos in a short book released some years prior.

Later in the same season of *Expedition Texas*, we decided to document a trip across Texas on Highway 80. The result was a series of three episodes we called "Expedition 80." We started in Waskom, Texas, at the Louisiana state line and followed the original alignment of the highway all the way to the New Mexico state line. We visited sites in East Texas, Terrell, Dallas, Abilene, Pecos and beyond.

We were able to find stories on several notable places on that trip and even explore a few of them. Much to our repeated disappointment, we had been trying to explore the Texas and Pacific Railroad Hospital in Marshall, Texas, since the inception of this show. The abandoned hospital building sits in a pitiful state just off Highway 80 in Marshall and has been frequently suggested as an expedition on our show by curious viewers. It isn't that we haven't tried. In fact, as the show was in development, I told many people about the concept to gauge feedback. The old T&P Hospital was first suggested by Steve Gomez, a business owner from Shreveport. He made the trip from Shreveport to Tyler frequently, and he had long wondered what stories that old building could tell. We made contact in the summer of 2012 with the owner of the property. He had once worked as the head of maintenance at the hospital and had somehow come to own the structure and the land it sat on. At that point, it was more a liability than a real estate investment, and the owner had a failing memory of what it all meant to Marshall. Over a weeklong series of calls, I tried to convince him to let us film an episode on the old hospital. Every time I called, I had to reintroduce myself, tell him again what the show was about and reexplain what we wanted to do. The kind old gentleman simply didn't understand, and permission was never granted. Over the later years, I'd occasionally poke around for information on the old hospital but never get very far. Now, it remains a curious site that always beckons me to pull over and take a photo every time I pass through. Years later, during the production of the Highway 80 tour episodes, we took some photos and video from the road—the closest we'd ever get to walking through those once-healing hallways.

In Terrell, Texas, Highway 80 is still a very vibrant stretch of road. Downtown Terrell is a center of commerce despite the plentiful shopping destinations along Interstate 20. In downtown, new businesses fill historic buildings, and the highway is known as Moore Avenue. A bodybuilder and professional wrestler named Calvin Knapp once operated his Hardbodies Gym in a historic building along this main drag. Calvin had married the daughter of a retired banker. Her name was Shawn Harris White, and upon Calvin's untimely death, Shawn managed the gym. She was keeping things running when we came through Terrell on our Highway 80 tour and allowed us to tour that historic building that we learned upon arrival had once been a hospital. Several features from those days could be found throughout the building. Doctors' offices lined the top floor, and patient rooms filled the middle floors. Our favorite feature was in the basement in an area we were told was the morgue. The young man who showed us the building worked for Shawn at the gym, and due to the quick nature of the Highway 80 tour episodes, we didn't check his research. We did, however, find one of his stories amusing, and a dutiful viewer later corrected it. We liked the guide's story better. At the back of the building near a set of stairs leading up to ground level was some sort of steep ramp going up to ground level as well. This ramp resembled a playground slide. The young man told us that the bodies would be delivered to the morgue down this little slide. We joked that it was like a night deposit drop for bodies. As our viewer corrected us, it was a way to gently remove the deceased from the morgue either on a gurney or in a coffin.

Beyond Terrell, where things get a little muddled along Highway 80, it became difficult to point to what was an original roadbed and what was a new spur. What was truly old Highway 80 gets extremely difficult to trace through Dallas, but we did make some stops to visit some known sites along the original route. One that resides along I-30 is the Grove Hill Cemetery.

Our stop there was simply to pay our respects to the First Family of Texas pro wrestling, the Von Erichs. David, Mike, Chris and Kerry Von Erich are all buried there.

In Pecos, Texas, we learned about the very first rodeo. As the story goes, the cowboys bragging over drinks about who could "out-cowboy" the others led to a competition between the men to determine who was truly the best. It was in tiny Pecos that a tradition was born, and a cowboy way of life was able to continue long after the days of cattle drives and twilight on the trail.

As we continued out west, the towns became fewer and farther between. Closer to New Mexico, more and more of the remnants of old towns appeared to be in ruins overrun by tumbleweeds. After nearly a week on the road, we stopped the car in Anthony, New Mexico, to shoot a little clip about finally crossing Texas on Highway 80. After such a long stretch on the road, stopping to shoot scenes throughout the trip, we were completely worn out. We did a couple of takes on the side of the road in Anthony, fell back into our seats, made a U-turn and appreciated the speed of the interstate all the way back to home base in East Texas. The ride itself was full of new discoveries and interesting bits of history. Had the trip not been combined with the significant work it took to shoot the episodes, it would have made a fantastic road trip vacation. The trip is now available as a DVD with all the episodes combined as a sixty-minute video, and the disc is busting at the seams with bonus clips from early unaired episodes about the highway.

Chapter 10

A BACKSTORY

I've always been fascinated with underground structures. When I was a fifth-grade student in Van, Texas, rumors circulated about underground tunnels that connected the old buildings on the campus. The school was built at the height of the Van Oil boom and was filled with extravagances afforded a rich oil town, so I was right to assume the rumors were true and made it my mission to open any unlocked door to see if it led below. There were locked doors that I suspected led to the tunnels, and I watched daily for them to be left opened. There was one blue door in particular that was always padlocked. It didn't connect to any classrooms, and I just knew it was the passage. The year passed, and I moved on to Van Junior High and couldn't roam that fifth-grade building after that—until high school!

In high school, I flourished in the theater arts program taught by Brenda Kellam. That program and her encouragement led to much of what you see me do to this day. Our plays were rehearsed and performed in the beautiful aging auditorium connected to the school and directly to that fifth-grade building. This auditorium was, in its heyday, a stately symbol of the wealth that the city once had and bestowed upon its children. Now, through years of decline, the building, like the dried-up oil wells around it, was falling into disrepair. Its beautiful, majestic structure was begging to be explored. During rehearsals for our one-act play competition, I'd find myself waiting backstage for my bit part to come up. I explored the old dressing rooms and storage areas with sixty years of accumulated odds and ends. One day, while the leads were taking an extremely long time learning their blocking, I ventured to the spotlight room in the back of the building. There was a small round opening in the ceiling, and I stacked chairs until I could lift myself through it. Unbeknownst to my teacher, I was high above her head walking on a wooden plank across the auditorium attic to the wall above the stage. If I had fallen through the ceiling, high above all those seats, it would have meant serious injury or death. What young man thinks seriously of such a risk? Looking back on it causes my heart to leap into my throat!

On another day of rehearsal, waiting for my tiny scene to come up, I rummaged through old set pieces behind the stage. I moved some flats to see what was behind them, and that's when I found an old wooden door. This back wall was the one that connected to the fifth-grade building! That building was the one where I always suspected there was an entrance to the mythical Van ISD tunnel. Maybe *this* door would lead to it! There was no padlock, just an old rusty doorknob. It took a little force and a bit of jimmying, but eventually it opened. I was ready to head down into the tunnel. I had a flashlight in my hand, and I was ready to use it, but as I looked down into the bottom of the doorway, I saw something I didn't expect. There was a pile of educational boardgames, new and still wrapped in plastic. There were letters of the alphabet freshly laminated. Shelves were stacked with a variety of things that would be used in a modern classroom. I was above the shelves looking down. I was in the top of a closet of some sort, and below me to my left was another door with light coming in under it. For some reason, I reached down as far as I could and knocked on that door. Imagine fifth-grade teacher Kathy Clanton's surprise when she heard a knock from *inside* her supply closet and, upon opening it, saw the confused face of Robert Mauldin dangling above the top shelf of her supplies! She was very startled. I apologized and scurried out of the opening and closed the door.

I tell this story because this is the origin of the appeal to what we do on *Expedition Texas*. I meet people all over the country who relate to the love of the mysteries these old buildings hold. For me, it started at a very early age trying to find those old tunnels. I later learned that they did exist. Older folks who grew up there remember them as tunnels where utilities ran between the many buildings on the campus and how maintenance workers were often accessing them. At the time I finally circled back and asked to explore them for this show, I was told they had been sealed off after multiple construction projects and prior to that were in standing water most of the time. None of the basements or underground areas we explored on *Expedition Texas* quite held the mystery of those tunnels—until we explored the Atlas Missile Silo…

Chapter 11

THE ATLAS MISSILE SILO

If you've driven out west, especially around Abilene, you have probably driven right past one of the most unusual underground structures to ever exist and never knew it. Imagine a field with a few random metal structures on the ground and a lone steel doorway. Like something out of a video game, you open the door to reveal a long staircase leading down, far beneath the surface. This place is real, and we went there to get the story.

It may have seemed like science fiction in the 1950s when they were developed, but Intercontinental Ballistic Missiles were the latest defense technology and by the 1960s could be launched from anywhere in the United States and travel up to 8,500 miles, landing within 1,500 yards of their intended target. The structures needed to house and operate these massive missiles were substantial, and for security reasons, they were all concealed underground. Dyess Air Force Base in Abilene planted these silos all around the Abilene area, and we were able to visit one in Lawn, Texas, with its current owner and historian, Larry Sanders.

Larry became enthralled with the concept of these massive underground structures and had made it his purpose to visit as many of them as he could around Abilene. One day, while Larry was giving an economic development talk in Lawn, the town's mayor approached him and asked why he hadn't visited their silo. So they traveled just a short distance out of town, and Larry found what was to be his pet project moving forward. All his work and research led to this spot and this moment in time, when he had the chance to purchase one of the silos and pursue a dream of turning it into a place where future generations could come to learn about the Atlas Missile Program.

The historical marker at the Atlas Missile Silo near Lawn, Texas.

Atlas Missile Silo information sign near Lawn.

We met Larry at the site on a hot summer day and sat under the shade of his hatchback SUV to talk about the history beneath our feet. There were features all around us in the tall weeds that had great significance to the mission. First, Larry made it clear that all the technology used and the weapons created were designed to be deterrent and that the true measure of success with a deterrent weapon is that you never have to use it. They never did. Near our parking spot was a small opening in the ground, framed in cement with a hatch that was made to open from underneath. Larry explained that this was the telescoping radio antenna designed to deploy should the permanent antenna that stood nearby be destroyed by an enemy. If the main antenna took a hit, this one would emerge and keep communications alive.

Another concrete base held another technical feature of the operation. A 180-foot piece of ten-inch pipe that descended into the operations room of the base was precisely aligned so that the North Star would always be visible through it. A device at the end of the tube would use this alignment to program the missile's inertial navigation system with the coordinates that allowed it to travel great distances with the accuracy mentioned previously. This was truly amazing technology in an era that predated GPS by decades.

A large cement disk, large enough to be the foundation for a house, covered an area of the ground where the missile was stored. Immense steel doors in the center were designed to open upon deployment of the missile. The missile would rise from the earth pushed by powerful hydraulic cams and sit in the ready position to await the call detonation from far below. Though it was never fired at a target, these weapons were always ready to defend our nation. Their deterrent mission was a success.

Probably the most fascinating aboveground feature was one that reminded me very much of a video game favorite from the 1980s. In *Super Mario Bros. 2*, you exit levels by going through a simple door that appears in a field with a slanted structure behind it, indicating that it leads below. This very thing sat as the only significant structure that you could see above ground level. A slanted cement box gave way to a steel door. With the turn of Larry's key, we opened the heavy door and proceeded to walk down one of the longest straight stretches of stairs I had ever traversed—far below the West Texas terrain and into the Launch Control Center for this Atlas Missile site.

At the bottom of the stairs there is a ninety-degree turn leading to the first of two one-ton manganese steel doors designed to protect the crew in the event of an attack above. Curiously, the door was easy to maneuver thanks to the superior design of its hinges. The first room we entered was

Top: Cement base for a sight tube at the Atlas Missile Silo.

Bottom: The entrance to the underground operations of the Atlas Missile Silo.

known as the "ready room," where the crew could work but also escape in the event of nuclear annihilation on the surface. Should the site be bombed, the traditional entrance with the door and long stairway would be destroyed, leaving the crew needing an alternative. An escape hatch, rigged with a cable, could be opened from the center of the room. The hatch would be full of sandbags that would absorb the initial blast and then fall to the floor upon triggering the hatch. The crew could then climb the ladder in the hatch to the surface to make their escape. This is a frightening scenario that

This page, top: A heavy door protected personnel from attack.

This page, bottom: An escape hatch leads personnel out of the underground control room in the event of an attack.

Opposite, top: The ladder leading out of the underground control room at the Atlas Missile Silo.

Opposite, middle: A tiny boat floats in the groundwater far below the surface in the silo.

Opposite, bottom: A view of the boat from a railing near the top of the silo. This cavernous hole in the ground once held an enormous missile.

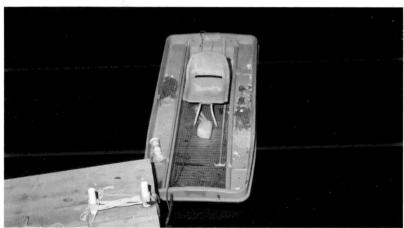

fortunately was avoided due to the deterrent power of the gigantic missile housed in the nearby eighteen-story silo.

Down more stairs and through a tunnel was the deep, dark home of the missile itself. This underground structure is as deep as the tallest building in nearby Abilene. With the aid of some lights Larry rigged in the silo, we could see far below, as water had filled the base. A small boat floated alone in the depths of the silo. My curiosity caused me to ask Larry why the boat was there. He replied that it was personal.

Looking down at the boat and into the darkness of the areas outside of the space illuminated by our lights, Larry reflected: "One of the loneliest feelings I've ever experienced is to be in my boat, adrift, floating the silo surface. Echoes. Dripping sounds. It's a tremendous escape. You are *extremely* alone, whether you are meditating or just hanging out on your boat in the silo."

Most of us will never know the feeling of isolation floating eighteen stories beneath the earth in pitch darkness, alone with our thoughts. Call it one of the few perks of owning your own 1960s missile silo in the middle of West Texas.

Chapter 12

DOOLE, TEXAS

On a hot Texas afternoon, the homework is done and stuffed into my green backpack for school the next day. I have an appointment with an imaginary family. *The Brady Bunch* comes on TV at 4:00 p.m., and I'll spend the half hour pining over Marcia Brady, not realizing that because this is a rerun, the actress who played her is old enough to be my mother. It's the ghost town episode! Yes! I love this one—and it's this episode that is partially responsible for a passion far greater than that one for Marcia, Marcia, Marcia! This episode made me fall in love with the idea of ghost towns.

The idea of a ghost town is cemented into the minds of American TV viewers by the rundown Old West imagery presented in shows like *The Brady Bunch* and by numerous tourist traps in Arizona and New Mexico. When you search for ghost towns in Texas, you'll usually find a few crumbling buildings that leave no clue as to what they were in life. You are also very unlikely to end up in the town jail, held captive by an old '49er looking to protect an undiscovered treasure. That's the fairy tale of a ghost town. The real thing has far less character and in some cases is just plain boring. Still, the romanticized version of ghost town, should it exist, was always a goal for *Expedition Texas*.

If you were passing through Doole, Texas, you'd see a few rundown structures, a beautiful old country church falling into ruin and perhaps a deer carcass, a victim of a hurried motorist. Doole, unlike a lot of ghost towns our viewers have suggested over the years, has something that is worth the trip to see. Reminiscent of the ruins of the Colosseum in ancient Rome, there is a baseball stadium back off the road in Doole, obscured by vegetation, that has fallen into ruin. We're not talking about aluminum bleachers and a press box here. This place has cement benches all the way across the backstop and a stairway that leads to the seats down in the bowl. A stone ticket booth perched at the top of the hill stands intact. We knew we had to go there.

A typical *Expedition Texas* shoot starts with some easy online research. We saw a few photos and could gather that there were still a few things to see in Doole, even though that abandoned baseball stadium was our main draw. The only active business there was a United States Postal Service outpost of sorts that was only occasionally staffed by whomever happened to want to volunteer, it seems. Figuring we could keep calling and eventually find the person in charge, we put Doole on our shoot schedule. Surely someone at the Doole Post Office knew someone who could show us around. Our producer kept calling. Thinking I'd have better luck, I started trying to call—as if my random call was any more important than Chris Moore's random call.

We began a weeklong shoot schedule with a day set aside to visit Doole. We tried repeatedly to reach the only seemingly occupied place in the little town—the United States Post Office, for crying out loud! Still nothing. So, I made a decision I expected would result in a costly waste of time and fuel. We drove to Doole, Texas, with no contacts, no real knowledge of what remained and nearly zero chance of making a coherent episode out of our travels.

You probably wouldn't believe this from watching the show, but I tend to be overly cautious. I hate the idea of bothering anyone, causing a disturbance and, especially, being shot at. I have this rule with our camera operators. They all know to keep rolling no matter what happens. If something happens to me, they are to get the shot *first*, then check on me. After several accidents that would have made great TV, I imposed that rule thinking that at best, we'd have some cool action shots. At the very worst, we'd have evidence. Traveling into an unknown ghost town and knocking on doors seemed dangerous and unprofessional, but I had to get this episode somehow. It's for that reason that cameras were pretty much rolling the entire first hour or so that we piddled around Doole. I half expected a shotgun blast through an unopened door to take me out. Sadly, though, we didn't even get an answer. This really was a ghost town.

I decided to go back to the little post office and leave a note. Maybe someone would eventually call, and if we were still on the road, we could circle back through. As we rolled up into the little drive, I noticed that at the old house next door, two old farmers were having a chat over the front fence.

I zipped right up to them in the car. Camera operator Sean Bloch started rolling. I hopped out and told him to follow.

Bill Lopez wore a black cowboy hat and kindly greeted me as I approached. The sight of the camera must have scared off the other farmer because he simply faded away from our conversation. The camera rolled as I asked Bill a couple of questions. Bill was infinitely knowledgeable on the area around us. He had grown up in Doole. He told us we could explore anything we wanted to explore because he knew everyone who owned land there, and we'd be fine. That still sounded like a recipe for getting shot, so I asked Bill multiple times to be our guide on the show and give us a short tour.

No. No. No. He tried to call someone named Briggs Browning. Briggs was in San Angelo buying feed. Maybe another day, boys.

I don't know how many times he told us he wouldn't be our guide before he ended up putting me in the back of his old truck and being the most hospitable and informative guide we've ever had on the show. Bill had a great time with us that day, and we had a great time with him! He took us into an old house adjacent to a mechanic's shop. The shop had various tools and car parts still scattered around, but repairs hadn't been made in this shop in decades. The owner of the shop lived in the house next door. The house easily dated back to the 1920s, and there were several signs of the life it once lived scattered about. The kitchen was added much later, and it held many clues about the period when the family lived in the house. A World War–II era jigsaw puzzle had been completed and hung near the back door leading out of the kitchen. Bill was amazed that it was mostly still put together and hanging on the wall where the proud family member had placed it for everyone to see.

Next, Bill took us to see the old country church. In the church were perfectly preserved pews, dried-out hardwood floors and the baptistry. As we explored, Bill said, "I think I'm gonna tear this down next week and use the lumber for a barn."

My heart sank a little bit. It was such a beautiful church, but it wasn't in use, and Bill saw an opportunity to make good use of the lumber. We're not sure if he ever made good on his plans for the church. We asked if we could keep the attendance sign that had been thrown into a back room and was covered in mud dauber nests. Bill let us keep a few souvenirs along the way. That was one of our favorites.

Next to the old church was a tiny building. The little shack didn't draw our attention until Bill pointed it out and said that it was the old telephone office for the town. It no longer housed the switchboard, but I can't picture it having that many switches, as the town didn't appear to have more than a few hundred residents even at its peak. We poked around in the little two-room building but didn't find anything to give hints about its previous existence.

We continued down the road to the feature of the old town that had brought us halfway across the state. The old baseball stadium sat off the main road at the edge of town obscured from view. Near the entrance was a metal building that was locked up tight. It was the community center, and Bill had a key. Inside, we found a goldmine of old photos, including photos of Bill, this Briggs Browning fellow and the baseball stadium in the early days. After thumbing through memories of Doole when it was a vibrant farming community that was full of life, we felt so much more connected to the town as it once stood. We had met only Bill, but thanks to his memories, we now knew more of the local players and the folks who made up the town. We even got to know this Briggs Browning we kept hearing about through the old photos and the stories that had been told to a much younger Bill Lopez.

As we stepped back outside into the bleakness of the overgrown terrain, there was a warning from Bill about not stepping on rattlesnakes. Heeding that warning became top priority as we found our way to the ruins of the old stadium.

The old ticket booth was in decent enough shape that it could still be used today, but just beyond it, where the fence used to surround the baseball stadium, things became more and more crumbled. We descended carefully down what used to be stairs into the seating area of the stadium. This area was full of jagged, crooked and broken cement slabs that once were benches. Bill seemed to go back in time. I could tell by the sly smile and the glimmer in his eyes that he was imagining the place from his childhood. He was seeing himself up to bat and the pretty girls cheering for him to hit a home run. That's one of the nice side effects of being a guide on our show: you get to relive the past and share it with the world. Bill opened his heart more and more.

Just as we wrapped what we thought was our entire shoot for the Doole episode, Bill got a phone call. He opened his flip phone and said, "Hellooo, Briggs! Yeah, they're still here. We'll be right over." Back into the bed of Bill's truck we went and down the road we traveled to Briggs Browning's house for a sit-down interview about Doole, Texas.

My favorite moments on *Expedition Texas* are the ones when we strike a nerve with our guides and see them completely transported back in time. It happened twice in this episode. That moment with Bill in the baseball stadium was the first, but the most impactful to me was when ninety-year-old farmer Briggs Browning shared his memories of the place where he was born and raised. As his mind raced down memory lane, we saw tears come to his eyes. The chills that came over our crew while talking to him in his home both put us at ease and made us grow up a little bit. Anyone of a certain age can look back on life and long for a bygone era. Briggs Browning spoke of how life revolved around this town. He told us how Doole was the center of life as he knew it. He found happiness there. He found love there. He made a life there. And not too long after we aired our favorite episode of the season, about Doole, Texas, he died there. He was ninety-three.

Doole, Bill Lopez and Briggs Browning will always hold a special place in our hearts.

Chapter 13

WHERE THE "OLD" ROAD LEADS

If this chapter comes across as more of a how-to guide for exploring your own area, then I'll feel like we've accomplished something here. This chapter isn't so much a story as it is a recommendation. However, it starts with a story.

In the days before GPS was on every mobile device, we relied on maps. Then, with the advent of MapQuest.com and sites like it, we could chart out trips on real interactive maps. Driving in the town where I lived and worked, Tyler, Texas, I was always curious about Old Omen Road. There was an outlying community called Omen. It wasn't even what you'd call a ghost town. Nothing was there. As far as I knew, Old Omen Road was a road within the city that had no connection to that small outlying community. I tried to research the community of Omen. This was long before I had ever entertained the idea of *Expedition Texas* and was looking into this out of my own curiosity. I learned that Omen had originally been called Canton and then Troup, losing its name to already established nearby communities. So, for whatever the creepy reason, it became Omen. Playing around on MapQuest.com in its infancy, I began to follow the line of Old Omen Road and zoomed in so I could recognize cross streets. As I kept clicking the little arrow to go up, suddenly the lines for roads on a white background were replaced with solid blue. I zoomed out. Old Omen Road led straight into Lake Tyler East. At first, my thought was that this road was incorrectly named, but I quickly realized that it was possible that the road predated the lake in existence. I zoomed out further. On the other side of Lake Tyler

East, the road picked back up. It had another name out there, but it was a road that picked up directly across the lake from where Old Omen Road ran straight into the water. The other road went directly to the tiny ghostly community of Omen. I proceeded to drive the route many times on long lunch breaks and got to know that area of East Texas well. I couldn't spot where the college once stood. Only a few homes remained in Omen.

Just in Tyler alone, there were many more "old" roads. Old Troup Highway was an alignment of road that led from Tyler to Troup, Texas. I'll give you a few guesses where Old Jacksonville, Old Noonday and Old Bullard went. In almost every case, the hands of time have erased sections of these roads, but you can still find alignments along the way, and if you can picture yourself in an old 1939 Ford, you can picture a trip from Tyler to one of these outlying cities. You can do this very thing where you live. For years now, I've used my lunch break or a Sunday drive with my family to follow the "old roads," and I've never been disappointed.

Following the "old road" came in extremely handy during our "Expedition 80" episodes, when we found ourselves leaving the interstate many times to get back on the trail of the old Texas Mother Road. Even in East Texas where marked sections of Highway 80 still exist, we would see signs for "Old Highway 80" and take those detours for some historic insight. Even farther down the line near Eastland, Texas, brick portions of the old Bankhead Highway offer an even deeper look into history.

It isn't feasible for most to go strolling into old buildings as we do on *Expedition Texas*. What is feasible is to load up the family on a Sunday afternoon, have one of the passengers pull up the story online and go on an adventure following the "old road." You never know what you're going to find. Just be careful not to drive off into the lake!

Chapter 14

BRECKENRIDGE YMCA

A silver-haired lady walks with a cane across warped boards of an old gym floor and reflects on her memories of sock hops, swimming lessons and first dates. She points to a small section of bleachers where she and her friends used to wait for the boys to ask them to dance. She doesn't realize she's doing it, but she begins to sway. For a blissful moment, she's wrapped in the arms of that farmer's son who was too shy to ask her himself but found a way, almost by accident, to touch her hand near the punch bowl and guide her onto the dance floor. Fifty years, a few kids and a small army of grandkids later, she stands where it all started and tells us the stories of this place—the way she remembers it.

If you've ever wondered why we spend considerable resources to travel across this state and explore these old places, it isn't for the love of exploring, period architecture, spider bites or dirt; it's for the stories. Every one of these old buildings has a story to tell. If you come with the right person, they almost take you with them back in time to the place in their memories. In their memories, the gym floor is polished to a sheen, those bleachers have a fresh coat of mint green paint and the music drifts like the echo of a thousand doo wop–singing angels.

Forgive me for being a bit poetic. I've just rewatched our episode on the Breckenridge Texas YMCA.

I had never heard of Breckenridge, Texas. Little did I know that the largest building in town was the one we were set to explore. An old familiar excitement crept in as we approached the building. We had an uneventful

The YMCA building at Breckenridge, Texas.

trip thus far, and nothing really stood out as "premiere-worthy" or "finale-worthy" for the episodes we had shot. I thought the building might be amazing, but the road-weary traveler's mind took over as we began to set up for the shoot. I became a little annoyed by the number of people who showed up. Once a shoot is underway, I'm the director, so I must figure out how all the players fit in. There were too many here. I didn't know what to do with them. Outside of one guide on an episode, others don't really help with the story. I don't like admitting this, but I wasn't in the best of moods starting this story.

As it turns out, word had gotten out about our arrival, and a lot of the people who showed up had memories of the building they wanted to share. Once my blinders lifted, I was able to see just how much this old building meant to the entire community in Breckenridge. This was an oddity to say the least. Usually, we must search for someone with enough knowledge or care about an old building to want to tour it with us. Here, we had teachers, librarians, the mayor and high school students who raised money to help restore it. I told the guys to set up to interview them all. While they were assembling cameras and adjusting lighting, I gave myself a walking tour of the building, reevaluated the situation and cooled my jets a bit.

It seemed that around every corner I turned on my self-guided tour, I found more and more to get excited about. There was that warped gym floor, a huge indoor swimming pool, multiple meeting rooms, locker rooms and some locked doors that I needed to peek into.

I came back downstairs more eager than before to explore the building and hear about the memories that were bound to be shared. Upon sitting down and really taking time to talk to everyone, I heard so many stories. We filmed so much more than would ever fit in a typical episode, but hearing those stories motivated me to tell this story better than any other we had told on this trip. Those sock hops, those after-school programs, the swimming team, the efforts of students who were too young to have known the building's history but still working so hard to restore it—it all gave me motivation to roam those halls and tell the story, because now, I wanted to hear it, too.

Breckenridge sits in Stephens County, Texas, as its county seat. The mayor, Bob Sims, was present for our shoot and became our primary guide for this episode. He's the kind of guy you'd want to sit and hear stories from on a hunting weekend somewhere, so to hear him talk about the Breckenridge YMCA building was a real treat. Jokes came up in almost every scene we shot. In one shot, he was telling us about the TV room where teens could cozy up and watch TV after a long day of school. He said that room had to be monitored extra closely so that the boys and girls didn't get *too* cozy!

As we explored the gym, Sims pointed out features no longer in existence and joked that all it needed to be like new again is…money. Down the hall and through some dressing rooms, we found the enormous pool. There was nothing wrong with the pool, but the heating bill to keep it warm year-round and to completely filter 100 percent of the pool water every twenty-four hours was more than the city wanted to pay, so it was shut down.

The costliest repair? The roof. One viewer on YouTube pointed out, "That building is a treasure but abandoned buildings that size always seem to die from the price of a roof. The costs are staggering, and most people give up before they get started. I'll guarantee that to use this building will require a start over with the plumbing and the wiring. The price tag just keeps getting bigger and I am cheering for anyone willing to try to raise the money to save it."

As we explored, we found rooms to let, three dollars per night, and shared space for a shower and toilet. Of course, you had a nest or two for some variety of bird. Our favorite spot, as always, was the basement level. It was, in the words of Mayor Bob, a "dark old creepy basement" where he had made "more trips than he cared to count" down some stairs that didn't really seem to be attached to anything. There were water mains and a furnace in that dark basement—all unused for decades.

The cleanup of the bottom floor by local high school students is proof positive that there is still love for the old building, and with a little luck and a whole lot of love, the building will see active life again soon.

Chapter 15

THE BALLAD OF
THE CUTHAND KID

Somewhere on a reel of Super 8 film, there's a clip of three boys unloading fishing poles and BB guns out of the back of an old Chevy. There's a jump cut, and the boys are crossing an iron bridge walking eagerly toward the perfect spot where they'll reel in a big one. There's another jump cut, and now we see the faces of Wade, Robert and Derrell Mauldin. Their father, Thomas Mauldin, has brought them to this spot near the old Mauldin homeplace in the tiny community of Cuthand, Red River County, Texas. In case you are wondering, Robert Mauldin is my father. Wade and Derrell are my uncles. Thomas—or, as his friends called him, Tommy—is my grandfather.

On either side, that iron bridge meets a dirt road that leads into and out of Cuthand. It's pronounced "cut hand" because local lore attributes the name to an injury some settler sustained in the early settlement there. It sounds like a joke a Mauldin would tell, and it is plain Mauldin dumb luck that the name would stick and be plastered on signs and maps throughout history. Either way, that's the name of this place. Cuthand.

Beside that reel of Super 8 film, in a box of things distributed among the grandkids after Tommy's passing, there are photos carefully scanned and meticulously preserved on CDs. There are enough of these photos to fill an entire stack of the CDs. Tommy was a technically savvy seventy-something great-grandfather before technology finally started to pass him by. This is why, when he was able, he maintained a database of Mauldin kin and a family tree so detailed that it would make a royal family envious. He also

Left: Tommy Mauldin on his horse near his family's barn in Cuthand, Texas.

Below: A family painting of the old homeplace at Cuthand hangs on Tommy Mauldin's wall during our visit.

Tommy Mauldin holds his grandson Robert "Bob" Mauldin Jr. in 1978.

kept those photos digitally stored and named with descriptive file names so that anyone coming along later could easily see who they portrayed.

One disc in particular contained scans of what seemed to be very old photographs. In some, a scrappy kid with a sly grin sports oversized overalls and close-cropped dark hair. Tommy was old enough by this time to have helped out with the daily chores at the old Mauldin homeplace in Cuthand. He helped toss loose hay in the loft of their barn to store it for winter feeding of the livestock. He gathered eggs and rode horses. They really didn't come more "country" than Tommy Mauldin, or anyone else who grew up in Cuthand for that matter.

By the time I was old enough to really pay attention to who my grandfather really was, his energetic days of hunting and fishing had passed him by. When I was young and we got together as family, I was more concerned about playing with my cousins. As an adult, I really started to listen to his stories as he'd thumb through album upon album containing the thousands of pictures he had scanned and stored digitally and then printed as large as he could so they'd fill his notebooks. He had photos dating back to the 1800s of family members who had first settled here. He also made a point to learn their stories through his own research.

Nothing transports you back in time more than the miniature farm he had constructed out of tiny wood slats and kept on display in a curio cabinet he built for my grandmother. In it were replicas of the old Mauldin house at Cuthand, the barn where he'd toss that loose hay, the old country church and even the family's outhouse, complete with a little plastic figure of a man on the seat doing his business. My grandfather dabbled in all sorts of hobbies, but preserving family history was his favorite.

When I was just shy of my teens, on a trip to nearby Bogata to visit my grandparents, my dad wanted to show us the old iron bridge where that home movie was filmed. We drove out to Cuthand and took off down that old bumpy road headed toward the Sulphur River. We followed the road all the way to Highway 271 in Johntown but never saw the iron bridge. Dad was confused, so we went back the opposite direction. He was sure he had the right road. They had been there a thousand times. But as he traveled the road this time, he was uncertain. As we approached the river, we crossed a nice, seemingly new cement bridge over the deep river below. Our best guess at the time was that the iron bridge had been removed to make way for the new cement structure.

Later on, in 2011, as an adult with my own family, I took my kids to visit my grandfather, their great-grandfather. During our visit, the conversation turned to Cuthand, and I asked him about that iron bridge and was surprised to learn from him that it had not been taken down. They had simply turned the road, made a new bridge and bypassed the original bridge. Immediately after that visit, I took the kids out to the old Cuthand road and drove to where the newer bridge crossed the river. I backtracked to a spot just before the river where the road made a sharp curve. Sure enough, just beyond a heavily overgrown ditch was a crumbling stretch of blacktop road. We hiked the traces of the old road about a quarter mile until we came to a washout. Once we carefully crossed the washout, we were able to find the old iron bridge over the Sulphur River. Over time, the erosion of the rapidly moving river had moved the banks out away from the edge of the bridge, and not a single plank of the wooden surface remained. Fortunately, from the side we approached, you could still reach the structure. I was able to let the boys sit on one of the beams and take their photo.

Bob's sons on an early hiking adventure that inspired *Expedition Texas*. *Left to right*: Ryan Mauldin, Trevor Bradshaw, Jacob Mauldin.

A year later, I was working on the concept for *Expedition Texas* and decided to do a story on the lost iron bridge at Cuthand. The abandoned structure fit the concept of the show perfectly. I approached my grandfather about doing the episode with us. He was reluctant at first but made a perfect guide for one of the very first episodes. We traveled out to Cuthand, and he made the hike with us along the bumpy, jagged remnants of the abandoned portion of the roadway. When we finally arrived, he proudly proclaimed for the camera, "There it is! The old iron bridge at Cuthand."

Most who travel the Cuthand road would never know that just around the river bend from the cement bridge there is an iron bridge that's lost to time. The locals know it and remember it, and surely, they have taken time to explore it for themselves. Driving around with Grandpa Mauldin that day, we heard stories about his childhood there. He pointed out the home of the old moonshiner at Cuthand who would "cook that moonshine comin' and a'goin' down in the river bottom."

The last time Grandpa Mauldin went to Cuthand, we found the land where the old homeplace once sat. It had been a goal for me to find it before he passed, and for some reason, on that day, riding with my wife and me, he was able to clearly guide us to it. We found the land quickly. We drove past the portion of the road where the bridge had been bypassed but didn't stop to explore. This time, he was far too feeble to make the hike. But he did enjoy the ride. In fact, we asked him several times if he was ready to go home. He wasn't. We rode and rode until he was finally tired enough to want to head back to Bogata.

In that old box of film reels and photos entrusted to me to preserve after his passing, I sometimes dig through and find those photos of that kid with the sly grin and oversized overalls. On one such trip down that proverbial memory lane, I was inspired to write a song about Tommy Mauldin called "The Cuthand Kid." On the recording of the song, three generations of Mauldin boys sing along, as I was joined by my dad, Robert, and my sons, Jacob, Ryan and Clay. The song was featured in tribute at the end of an episode of the show.

> *Down by the Sulphur River across that old iron bridge,*
> *Sits the old homeplace where they raised the Cuthand Kid.*
> *He may have went to the big city, but his heart never did.*
> *And of all the places he's roamed,*
> *This country is still the home,*
> *Of the Cuthand Kid.*

I think of all those family visits as a kid when I was more concerned about playing outside with my cousins and the hundreds of times I walked past that curio cabinet with replicas of his homeplace and wish I knew then the types of stories they could tell. Every family has them. Some took place in the city, and some took place out in the country. Some took place

Bob Mauldin explores the abandoned iron bridge at Cuthand on one of our first episodes of *Expedition Texas*, taped in 2012.

in a different country. But every family has a story. If I can communicate anything to you in this story of the Cuthand Kid, it might be to slow down, take time and listen. Your family has its own lost legends and places to explore that connect you to where you came from.

Chapter 16

BARRY CORBIN

What is the number-one question we receive online about our show? Address of a building? No. Name of a guide? No. Who designed those impressive outfits worn by your host? Definitely, NO!

The number-one question we receive on our website and social media is, "Who is that voice on your show intro?"

That's reasonable. His voice is one of the most recognizable in film and TV, and when we sought him out to provide a voiceover for our show open, we never in a million years thought that he would agree. But he did, and now we have one of the most recognizable voices in film and TV on our show every single week.

My introduction to Barry Corbin probably came the same way the rest of the world came to know him. In his first movie role, he portrayed "Uncle Bob" to John Travolta's "Bud" in the classic *Urban Cowboy*. If you can watch the scene where Uncle Bob lectures Bud on pride and then dies a short time later in an industrial accident and you do not shed a tear, you may have been born without a heart.

In fact, this set up a trend of Barry Corbin characters delivering profound lines in hit movies. In *War Games*, he proclaims that he'd "piss on a spark plug," and much later, in *No Country for Old Men*, he talks about how an uncle "met his reward." As recently as his portrayals of salty characters in *Yellowstone* and *Tulsa King*, Barry has delivered performances that are brief but memorable. On the TV front, his character "Ed" in *Anger Management* has been hilarious comedy relief in every single episode. He played the recurring character of a coach in *One Tree Hill* and somehow managed to be despised by audiences who loved that show.

We don't see how anyone could despise a Barry Corbin character, but if they do, it's only because it is so well acted that you fall for whatever character he's seamlessly inhabited. We didn't know which Barry Corbin we'd meet when we stopped by his place in March 2015 to record the new intro for *Expedition Texas*. On that day, we were a little nervous. We had just been at Bill Mack's house recording interviews for an episode about his career, prior to heading to Shamrock, Texas, to explore locations associated with his early days in radio. I had some communication with Barry's daughter prior to our Fort Worth trip, and I knew that Barry might be interested in helping us out. When I mentioned this to Bill Mack, he told me that Barry didn't live far from him, and he had been to his house many times. This prompted me to text Barry's daughter to see if we could swing by to record the voiceover for the show. Barry was home from filming at that time, and she told us to come on by.

After that conversation, with the knowledge that the quality of our show was about to shift dramatically, I stopped by the pharmacy on the way and picked up a thank-you card and the most expensive bottle of wine I could find: $12.99. Francis Coppola cabernet. It was named after a famed movie director. Couldn't go wrong, right? He probably gave it to the pool boy.

We arrived at Barry's house. In my head, I felt that he must be doing this out of charity for us and wanted to get it over with. I devised the quickest way to record the lines possible. I found out within the first few minutes of meeting Barry Corbin that I did not need to be nervous. He seemed honored to do this for us and chatted about his film work and talked to us about our show. He recorded several different versions of the lines for us, which we've alternated and used for the nearly eight years since he recorded them. Looking back on that day, there are some things that I still marvel about.

First, it isn't every average Joe who gets the opportunity to direct a legendary actor like Barry Corbin. I have often wondered if he sat there as I asked him to reread a line and thought to himself, "Who does this kid think he is?" or "That cheap wine better be good!"

Secondly, we were at his home. Pretty sure they didn't shoot any of his famous movie scenes at his house. When he did voiceovers for 99.5 KPLX in Dallas, he went to a proper studio. We had a microphone on a dining room table in a barn.

I walked away from that extremely cool encounter with some audio I needed to figure out how to use. Piecing together some of the best takes, I

Bob Mauldin directs actor Barry Corbin in the recording of the *Expedition Texas* show intro.

fashioned a set of show intros and commercial "bumpers" to use in the show. I've re-edited those things a few times over the years and keep using them, even as Barry Corbin went on to play roles in some amazing projects. I keep expecting a call from some mythical studio executive telling me to stop using Barry's voice. But that has never happened! In fact, in 2023, another Barry brought Barry Corbin and me back together.

Barry Rogers is the hardest-working publicist I've ever encountered. His work with a gaggle of celebrities led us to cross paths again in 2005, when he was representing the original Bo Duke, John Schneider, as he renounced the most recent Hollywood version of *The Dukes of Hazzard*. Barry Rogers handled this task like a champ, especially considering that John himself was making movies at the time that made the 2005 *Dukes of Hazzard* look like *Sesame Street*. (I started to write *Mister Rogers Neighborhood*, but Barry tires of those jokes quickly.)

Moving on, Barry was now representing Barry. It was Rogers's suggestion that *Expedition Texas* follow up with Corbin to see how he was doing and finally answer that age-old question: "Who is that voice at the beginning of your show?" We were happy to oblige, and this time we had secure confirmation from Barry Rogers that Barry Corbin was, too.

Barry Corbin (*left*)
and Bob Mauldin
(*right*) on a recent visit.

We circled the Corbin estate for about thirty minutes. You don't want to seem too eager to show up to these things, you know. The last time we were there, we only needed the voice. This time, we were hoping to visit with the man himself. We pulled into the driveway using the provided gate code and were met at the back entrance by an extremely kind lady we didn't recognize. This was Mrs. Jo Corbin. Jo and Barry had married sometime since our last visit, and I could tell in a moment that she was an absolute gem of a person. She lingered at the back of the production truck as if she wanted to carry in some equipment. I assured her we had it covered and proceeded to visit with her about Barry and the Mastiff puppies that his daughter raised. As we made small talk, the guys unloaded camera equipment. We might have brought a little more than needed since we were trying to film a movie legend.

After the guys unloaded the camera gear, Jo led us into the room where Barry was waiting in his cowboy-best duds and western boots. Barry welcomed us as any southern gentleman would welcome company. He was as friendly and accommodating as you could expect your grandfather to be when you come to visit after a long absence. We immediately felt at home, but I was soon faced with a new challenge.

Now, I not only had to tell a movie legend how to deliver a certain line; I was also telling him where to stand, directing cameras, motion, lighting and blocking. It was all jumbled. I just tried to not look like an idiot. This man had been in front of cameras under the direction of Martin Scorsese, the Cohen brothers and tons of other legendary directors, and here was good ol' Bob Mauldin, tellin' camera men Matt and Nyc to "point that one this way and that other one the other way."

Barry Corbin was an amazing guest. He showed us his cabinet full of awards. He introduced us to his father-and-son duo of Mastiff pups, and Jo even nursed Nyc back to 100 percent after a yellowjacket sting near the door to Barry's man cave.

Barry made a point to give us some cool new things to use on *Expedition Texas*. But in a show of extreme kindness, he also autographed photos to each of our fathers, as we were shooting the weekend before Father's Day. All the guys reported that the photos were a hit. For my dad, I bought the series *Lonesome Dove* on DVD, in which Barry portrays the loveable character "Roscoe."

"I can find Texas, Peach! But how do I find July?"

Oh, the greatness of that voice!

Especially when he says, "This is *Expedition Texas*…and we're gonna find it!"

Thank you, Barry Corbin.

Chapter 17

WHEN HOLLYWOOD
CAME TO TEXAS

The best way to give a Hollywood film about Texas that realism that so many directors look for is to shoot in the Lone Star State. It's a goal of many dabbling in production to someday produce a feature film. I'm one of those people. Texas offers so many inspiring backdrops and landscapes that the ideas come easily. Along with the incentives offered by the State of Texas, this is why so many film productions shoot in Texas.

In our first season, we visited the locations of the '70s horror film *Texas Chainsaw Massacre*. This started a trend in our show that we try to repeat often. It is exciting to visit locations we're familiar with from our favorite films, to point out where our favorite scenes took place and then go home and watch those movies with our friends. The *Texas Chainsaw Massacre* production originated in Texas with Tobe Hooper and young filmmakers working with him on the project. In the film, there are several locations that are still accessible and a few that are gone.

At the beginning of *Chainsaw*, the travelers find themselves at a gas station that also sells barbecue. During their visit, there is a man who attempts to wash their windows several times, and one of the girls fights with a soda machine. It's only a short scene, but the girl finds her way to the gas station again in the climax of the film, when she stumbles into the ghastly barbecue operation with the patriarch of the chainsaw family. In 2012, when we first shot our episode on the movie locations, the gas station located near Bastrop was abandoned and in very much the same condition as it appeared in the 1974 film. We were able to get shots of it from the road without having to

During a tour of New Republic Studios near Austin, Bob pilots a tank.

enter the property, adhering to our policy of never trespassing for a shoot. That weekend, we also met up with *Texas Chainsaw Massacre* movie expert Tim Harden to see Quick Hill. Most of the scenes at the farmhouse took place atop this hill north of Austin near Roundrock. A county road out front provided a setting for much of the action, including the finale of the film. Growth in the area around Quick Hill had it almost inaccessible. The new Austin Loop cut a chunk out of Quick Hill when it was built, and the farmhouse used in the film was relocated to Kingsland, Texas.

In 2012, we walked to the top of Quick Hill, and Tim Harden showed us where several key moments of the movie took place. We left that meeting with him and saw the cemetery used in the beginning of the film and then traveled to Kingsland to tour the original farmhouse. After its relocation, the house was repurposed to be used as a restaurant. The restaurant serves meals in the rooms used in the film, and the food is prepared in the very kitchen where Leatherface claimed many of his victims.

In 2022, we revisited many of the locations from our first season on the air as a tenth-anniversary season for the fall of that year. One major difference in the locations after all this time was that the gas station in Bastrop was now open for business in a way that fully celebrated its fame as a movie location. The Texas Gas Station, as it is now known, lets fans experience the location in new ways. A movie memorabilia shop inside the main building allows horror fans to celebrate their favorite films with action figures, posters, T-shirts and more. They also installed cabins at the back of the property so that brave overnighters can stay the night where the *Chainsaw* horror took place. To top it all off, they also serve delicious barbecue—which, according to our guide, is *not* made from humans!

The house that was moved to Kingsland was still in operation as a restaurant and served amazing food. We enjoyed our meal and interviewed a few patrons to see if they realized what the house was famous for. Probably the most disappointing location we visited during that anniversary shoot was the area once known as Quick Hill. The abandoned county road was still somewhat there if you knew what you were looking for. Of course, Tim Harden always knows how to find it, so he met us there. On the east side of the road, a high chain-link fence now spanned the abandoned chunk of road to the top of the hill. At the top of the hill, beyond the fence, the location where the house once stood in the middle of farmland had been graded for some sort of construction. Tim was able to point out some of the locations, but we could no longer walk the driveway up to where the house once stood. All of that was gone. A year later, in 2023, while working on this book, we drove past Quick Hill on that Austin Loop. A large building stands on the piece of land where the notorious film location once existed.

This area of Central Texas certainly attracts great films. The house used in the film *Hope Floats* sits in Smithville, Texas, and Bastrop is well known as a location-rich haven for film companies. We once toured a film studio near Bastrop and even drove a tank that had been used in movies shot there. Bastrop invited *Expedition Texas* to cover their Christmas festivities in 2022, and in a final scene, we walked along the Brazos River on a paved walkway with their historic iron bridge visible in the background. The following year, in a key scene in the series *Love and Death*, I spotted the familiar riverside walkway and the iron bridge in the background.

Chapter 18

THE COTTON OIL MILL
AT ELGIN

As I dug through the dirt and fire ants flinging potatoes into the rows, I wondered if there were easier ways to farm potatoes. Under what little protection a beat-up straw cowboy hat could provide, the sun burned my skin as Old Man Brickey barked at me from the fender of his blue Ford tractor to hurry it up. Mr. Brickey had farmed all the land that surrounded our little homeplace in Colfax since he was a young man. On this day, he was an old man, and I was just thirteen years old. It was my first real job. I was excited to be making my daily cash wage. Brickey's farm had declined from its booming operation down to just a few fields scattered across his land. He went from having a truckload of farmhands to having one neighbor kid needing a summer job. I had started my job for him learning how to pull onions from the ground. Then we moved on to the pepper patch, then the cornfield. This day in the potato field was the worst. Brickey plowed the row with that old tractor, turning up the potatoes and the fire ants. It was my job to go through the dirt and toss the potatoes into neat piles along the row. I moved as fast as I could, occasionally raking the stinging ants off my arm.

After that hard day in the field, we spread the potatoes in the barn on some fresh hay. Then, he paid me, and I rode home on my bike. The next day, Mr. Brickey wound up in the hospital, where he stayed for weeks. I don't recall his ailment, but I had to pursue other ways to make money that summer because his small farming operation shut down without the

Colfax is located along FM 16 between Van, Texas, and Canton, Texas, in Van Zandt County.

farmer in charge. Occasionally, just to help out, I'd feed his cows and move them from one field to the other. Those potatoes sat forgotten in that hay in the barn. When a weakened Mr. Brickey came home from the hospital, we rode out in his truck to the barn. He needed me to gather the now-rotted potatoes from the floor of the barn and help dispose of them. Now, I consider myself to have a strong stomach. I don't get grossed out easily at all, but a rotten potato has to be one of the worst smells I've ever encountered in my life. Thinking about that day as I write this, I can suddenly smell it again. I handled the potatoes as gently as possible so I wouldn't rupture the skin and get the gross contents all over my hands, but no matter how carefully I handled the taters, they would end up leaking their vile death juice all over my cotton work gloves. Others would seem to be still useable until a slight squeeze would cause the white, stinking funk inside to squirt out on my shirt. If digging potatoes in a hot field with angry fire ants was bad, this was far worse.

Cleaning out the barn of rotten potatoes was the last job I did for Mr. Brickey. I swore off the field hand work after that summer. But there was one very important thing that summer job did for me: it taught me to appreciate where our food comes from. I became a huge fan of eating and cooking with vegetables after that summer. I only knew a little about farming, but I developed a great appreciation for families who build their lives around the business of putting food on our tables. What I didn't yet understand is that farmers do much more than that.

In 2020, we were shooting episodes of *Expedition Texas* around a schedule that depended heavily on what the latest COVID-19 advice said we could do. We received word from producer Chris Moore that there was an old mill in Elgin, Texas, that would be a great location to explore and that he had lined up a guide and we'd get full access. So, we took off to visit Elgin, where I learned that I don't know much of anything about farming.

Cotton was king in Central Texas. Of course, cotton is used in many ways to make fabrics, but prior to the nineteenth century, cotton seeds were virtually useless and an annoyance to farmers trying to get a clean product to market. Of course, a good portion of those seeds was used to plant the crop, but the majority was left to rot or was illegally dumped into rivers. It

The Elgin Cotton Oil Mill in Elgin, Texas.

wasn't until Procter and Gamble began looking for alternative ingredients for candles that they began using cottonseed oil. Later, in 1899, cottonseed oil was developed for cooking by Wesson. Soon, more uses for cottonseed oil were being developed, and it became necessary for places like the Elgin Cotton Oil Mill to spring up near the cotton fields of the South.

The black land of the fields in and around Elgin is a prime environment for raising cotton. We're not talking about plantations and slave labor here. We're talking about poor families growing the very means to their existence. If you know anyone born before the 1960s in that area, you know that their childhood was centered on the entire family being in the fields picking cotton by hand. The children often had the job of "scrapping them bowlies," as Perryman called it, the hard, sharp shell that cotton comes from. Nothing was allowed to go to waste, not even the fine remnants left behind after the adults had almost picked the bush clean. I heard these stories from Tom Perryman, a man I mentioned earlier for his contribution to Elvis Presley's trips to East Texas, who had spent his childhood in a cotton field and swore it off in favor of a career in radio and country music at a young age. "Scrapping them bowlies" would leave a kid's hands torn up from the hard, sharp husk. Dragging a cotton sack down the rows left Tom with lifelong back problems. But that was life, and as I've said, cotton was king in Central Texas back then. Naturally, with the discoveries made in the uses of cottonseed oil, industry followed. The Elgin Cotton Oil Mill was a massive operation near a switch track off the main railroad line.

On rare occasions, we explore places where it seems time stood still. These places have hints of their story all around as you explore. There are times in places such as this that if you reintroduced the people and their jobs, things would continue just as they left off regardless of time and its effects. Grease a bearing, tighten a belt and flip the switch, and the work resumes. That's what makes our trip to Elgin so special. To them, it was an industry that had dried up. To us, it was a glimpse at one of the larges industries in the small town.

The Lundgren family settled in Elgin in the 1800s and until 2014 ran the cottonseed oil mill. Our guide, Brian Lundgren, worked at the mill his entire life. We met up with Brian at a nearby blacksmith shop and followed overgrown train tracks into the plant area. Even in areas where the buildings had long ago collapsed and been scrapped for lumber, artifacts remained. An old scale stood alone on a concrete slab. Nearby, a storage room filled with receipts and paperwork could single-handedly tell the story of the mill. But we continued to the large buildings that still stood at the heart of

Top: The entrance to the Elgin Cotton Oil Mill.

Bottom: All of the old machinery still remains at the Elgin Cotton Oil Mill.

Large machines pressed oil from cotton seeds at the Elgin Cotton Oil Mill.

the operation. In the main processing room was a giant dormant machine that was used to de-lint the seeds. It would remove the remnants of cotton attached to the seed and separate the outer hull from the kernel. The hulls were not wasted either; they found use as cattle feed roughage. The kernels were then cooked and sent through expellers that would squeeze out the oil within the seed. The kernels, minus most of their oil, would also be used as a supplement to feed cattle. The oil went on to its destiny—in your kitchen.

A nearby massive building was the storage facility for the raw product that was brought into the mill. Since we were touring the building from the end of the process to the beginning, we explored this bit last. There, we found remnants of the raw product and were able to see where the oil came from. As usual, I ventured into a place not seen in many years. High in the storage building was a vacuum-like piece of machinery that would remove the cotton seeds from the trucks and place them into their respective place for processing.

Our tour did not end there. The nearby office still had awards on the wall and computer floppy discs on the desks. One award read, "Voluntary Purchasing Groups, Incorporated recognizing Elgin Cotton Oil Seed Mill."

Multiple large desktop computers were scattered about, and there was a room with a coffee maker where several magazines were strewn. The *Sports Illustrated* Swimsuit Issue from 1979 featured Christie Brinkley.

In the back of his Jeep, Brian kept a few souvenirs of his days at the mill. Several promotional items such as calendars and magnets were preserved. A nearby cooler of cheap beer on ice brought relief after another tour of an abandoned building on a hot summer day.

Chapter 19

MARY ALLEN COLLEGE

About midway through the first season of *Expedition Texas*, we began to see the growth from being on TV, and the attention we were getting from viewers was all very positive. Almost immediately we began to receive tips from viewers about places we needed to visit. The show caught the attention of East Texas writer Dana Goolsby. Dana wrote about people and places in East Texas and had stumbled upon some great stories of her own and wanted to tell us about a few that she thought fit the show. Since planning for the second season started as soon as the first season ended, we were ready to start talking about more great stories to feature on *Expedition Texas*.

Dana's first suggestion was a set of corncribs in an old barn. Hard to make a full episode out of corncribs, but we still dedicated a segment to the cribs. The age and level of preservation was impressive, thanks in no small part to the fact that these corncribs had been under the cover of a well-built barn for their entire existence.

Next, Dana blew us all away with a trip to Crockett, Texas, to see Mary Allen Seminary. At the time, I completely took my guides' word that we were going to see something amazing, and there had been a few times I questioned their excitement. This was not one of those times. The moment I first saw the only remaining structure of Mary Allen Seminary, I knew it was something special. I didn't even know the story, but I knew I needed to tell it.

Many great horror films have some ominous structure that is a central character in the movie. As we rolled up the overgrown drive into the ruins of the Mary Allen campus, I felt like I was visiting a Hollywood set created

Mary Allen College in Crockett, Texas.

to strike fear among movie watchers. The architecture of the more-than-one-hundred-year-old structure had a Gothic feel to it. Atop towers at each end, buzzards perched looking for their next meal. Falling bricks littered the area surrounding the building, and it was obvious from the outside that one end of the building had internal structural damage. It would have been very easy to make the story about a creepy old building with some amazing architectural features. If I had done that, I would have overlooked one of the greatest stories we've had the privilege to tell on this show.

I learned early on that, despite the mood set off by a building, I need to let the story unfold as it may. Mary Allen was one of the earliest examples of that policy paying off in a great way. The campus we were here to explore was no regular college. Mary Allen Seminary had been created, under the encouragement and pressure of Mrs. Mary Allen herself, to be an institution of higher education for young African American girls just emerging from slavery.

In 1886, when the school was opened by Presbyterian pastor Richard Allen and his wife, Mary E. Allen, it was the only institution in the state opened to the more than 200,000 freed Black women in Texas. Mary had some influence over her husband during planning for the school, which began in 1883 by the Board of Missions for Freedmen of the Presbyterian Church. Richard was secretary of the board. Crockett was chosen for its large African American population at the time. Mary died in 1887, and the school was then named in her honor.

The school began by offering liberal arts education but, after some criticism, switched to offering real-world education in many of the trades offered to women at the time. All the students were Black despite the school having all white faculty and staff. This was to change as well, because in

The upper floor had collapsed onto the bottom floor of the main building at the college.

1924, the school appointed its first Black administrator, Reverend Burt Randall Smith. Smith set about the task of restructuring the college. He sought to overhaul the curriculum and have the college expand its library and science facilities. By 1932, the school had become an accredited junior college with an all-Black faculty. In 1932, it became known as Mary Allen College and became a coeducational school.

In 1943, the school failed to be recognized as an accredited Black state college and ended up closing shortly after. By 1944, a different organization had reopened the college, and it operated successfully in Crockett until its closure in 1972.

It is important to note that we were pulling into the driveway of a building that had been closed since 1972. It was November 2012, and the halls of the building had not seen life in that entire stretch of time. The building had been vacant for forty years. The land was overgrown for forty years.

We met our guides for the Mary Allen College expedition at the old side entrance of the building. In the sidewalk along this side of the building, a graduating class once signed their names. After taking in the nostalgic scribblings, we entered the side of the building. It didn't take us long to learn that our hike through the building would be protracted by the massive fallen upper floors and general debris everywhere.

Half of the building was still intact, for the most part. Looking down a long main corridor, we could see that beyond a beautiful winding staircase at the midway point in the building, the second and third floors now rested in splintered ruin on the first-floor level. We made our way down the portion of the hallway we could reach. As we carefully peeked into each room, we could see signs of school life by way of chalkboards and desks in each classroom. When we finally made it to that staircase in the middle, I found myself walking up, only to discover that the stairs were no longer attached, and my weight was more of a strain than they had seen in ages. I carefully walked back down. I hadn't torn up an *Expedition Texas* site yet, and I wasn't about to start on this trip. Access to the upper floors on the intact side of the building was instead gained by climbing the steel fire escape ladder at the back of the building. It's funny how in the early days, I'd climb anything or scurry down any hole to get a shot. This day, climbing to the second floor, I was told that this was where the girls at Mary Allen College would set up housing. These were essentially their dorms. Walking the halls, I could almost hear the giggles coming from behind the other closed doors. But there was another floor to see.

The third floor was accessible through the fire escape and out the back window I had just climbed up to. There was only one room on this end of the building that seemed sturdy enough to carry the weight of a man. I slowly crept out onto that floor, which connected gingerly to a nearby wall. Through that mostly destroyed wall, I could see the next room. There was no floor. A sink and mirror were connected to the brick wall, with no floor below, by only some aging plumbing. As I stood on that third floor slightly confused by the strange sights around me, I began to hear something falling beneath my feet. I realized that the items falling below me were pieces of the floor. The third floor was beginning to crumble beneath my feet, and I could hear the destruction of the floor I was standing on. Then, panic! In a mad rush, I scampered back to the window, out onto the fire escape and back down to safety.

As we explored the lower floor of the college, our guides told us of the grand plans to restore the old school to create a visitors' center and museum for Crockett. They also laid bare the reality of trying to do such a thing in a crumbling building in a financially strapped city in Texas. The most they could hope for would be a steel structure built within the façade of the old outer walls. They could possibly look at a building within a building, provided the outer structure would hold up. This seems unlikely noting the number of bricks and pieces of the outer structure that had found their way to the ground in recent decades.

The ladies who showed us around spoke with great reverence about Mrs. Mary Allen and the school she helped influence before her death. Because of her efforts and those of Mr. Allen, this school operated to serve the Black community, starting with those who had been held by the bonds of slavery and up through the generations, eventually serving those who had no idea the impact their ancestors had on the way they were able to achieve an education from an accredited college.

What started out as a place to learn a certain set of skills that would help in domestic life soon became a place where young African American girls could go on to earn degrees and earn their living and their place among leaders in the society we all live in and share.

Stories like that of Mary Allen College are the very reason we keep on hunting to find hints of Texas's colorful past. Our lost history.

EPILOGUE

Somewhere along the way, I decided that I'd keep producing this show as long as people seemed to want to hear the stories we found. Over the past decade, the support for what we do has only grown. We don't pay for followers on social media. The people you see keeping up with us are there because they really care about the stories we tell.

There have been times when my attention has been divided. Sometimes the need to take care of a growing and changing family trumps the need to make that trip to shoot new episodes. Sometimes a boy leaving home to join the United States Air Force diverts your attention for a few weeks.

Both of my older sons, Jacob and Ryan Mauldin, have worked on the show in some capacity. Both have been camera operators, but Ryan really hit a groove of working steadily on the show prior to going into the air force. Jacob, the oldest, has been pursuing auto mechanics. Both keep me abreast of great story ideas on a regular basis. Their little brother, Clay Mauldin, has his sights set on being famous someday. He's a heck of a singer and loves his dad's business.

In 2019, I married my sweet Tessa. She was with us on that Branch Davidian shoot and gained an honorary position on the crew when she unknowingly caused a continuity error in our episode on the Magnolia Hotel in Seguin, Texas, by suggesting that I tuck in my wrinkled shirt *after* filming the outside walk-up scene. This led to one of those moments where the host had his shirt untucked when he opened the door, but it was suddenly neatly tucked in when he entered the house.

This page, top: Bob tapes studio segments for *Expedition Texas*.

This page, bottom: *Left to right*: Jeff Miller on camera, Bob Mauldin and Jeff Stewart during an interview for the popular Bigfoot episode.

Opposite: Jason Garrett (*left*) and Bob Mauldin (*right*) take off on the road to shoot *Expedition Texas*.

Later, Tessa blessed me with something I never knew I needed—a daughter. Our Maggie Bell Mauldin was born during the pandemic in 2020 at a time when we were scared and confused like the rest of the world.

In 2023, I bought an old Ford Expedition. Seems fitting for a car that carries us on our "expeditions" across Texas. Maggie calls it my "Expedition Car." Now, so do I.

You see, down the road there's always another lost legend waiting to be explored. On *Expedition Texas*, we're gonna find it.

ABOUT THE AUTHOR

 **B**ob Mauldin has worked in radio and television for close to thirty years, dedicating the last decade of his career to telling the stories of Texas's colorful past by exploring lost history on TV's *Expedition Texas*. As host and producer, Bob traverses the state to find and explore abandoned buildings, ghost towns and other exciting locations with respect to their history. Bob produces a wide variety of TV programs through his company, 31 West Productions, in Tyler, Texas. He lives in Whitehouse, Texas, with his wife, Tessa, and their children.

Visit us at
www.historypress.com